Generously Donated by the Goodwyn Institute

MEMPHIS LIBRARY FOUNDATION

Wild Science
Careers

LAVA
SCIENTIST
Careers on the
Edge of Volcanoes

SARA L. LATTA

Enslow Publishers, Inc.
40 Industrial Road
Box 398
Berkeley Heights, NJ 07922
USA

http://www.enslow.com

Library of Congress Cataloging-in-Publication Data

Latta, Sara L.

    Lava scientist : careers on the edge of volcanoes / by Sara L. Latta.

        p. cm. — (Wild science careers)

    Summary: "Explores careers in volcano science using examples of real-life scientists"—
Provided by publisher.

    Includes bibliographical references and index.

    ISBN-13: 978-0-7660-3049-7

    ISBN-10: 0-7660-3049-7

    1. Volcanoes—Vocational guidance—Juvenile literature. 2. Geology—Vocational guidance—
Juvenile literature. 3. Volcanologists—Juvenile literature. 4. Volcanological research—Juvenile
literature. I. Title.

    QE34.L38 2009

    551.21023—dc22   2008004679

Printed in the United States of America

052010 Lake Book Manufacturing, Inc., Melrose Park, IL

10 9 8 7 6 5 4 3 2

To Our Readers: We have done our best to make sure all Internet Addresses in this book were active and
appropriate when we went to press. However, the author and the publisher have no control over and
assume no liability for the material available on those Internet sites or on other Web sites they may link
to. Any comments or suggestions can be sent by e-mail to comments@enslow.com or to the address on
the back cover.

Photo Credits: AFP/Getty Images, p. 99; AP Photo, p. 20; AP Photo/Pier Paolo Cito, pp. 1, 112; AP
Photo/Steve Young, p. 115; Christina Heliker, courtesy, U.S. Geological Survey, p. 34; Courtesy of the
U.S. Geological Survey, p. 75; Courtesy, Lucia Pappalardo, pp. 26, 29; Dave Huss/iStockphoto.com,
p. 24; Dave Sherrod, U.S. Geological Survey, p. 104; Dr. Robert Embley, NOAA, PMEL, OAR, p. 78; Gary
Hincks/Photo Researchers, Inc., p. 15; J.D. Griggs/U.S. Geological Survey, pp. 33, 39; Jacques Durieux,
___ __9; John Catto/Alpenglow Pictures, pp. 59, 60, 63; Mike Poland/U.S. Geological Survey, p. 8;
_____ /University of Arizona, pp. 46, 55; NASA/JPL-Caltech, p. 51; National Park Service, Jim Peaco,
_____ Pacific Ring of Fire 2004 Expedition. NOAA Office of Ocean Exploration; Dr. Bob
_____ Chief Scientist, pp. 72, 76, 84; Photo courtesy of Lisa Morgan, p. 88; Photograph
_____ Christiansen/U.S. Geological Survey, p. 40; R.P. Hoblitt, U.S. Geological
_____ _ Geological Survey, p. 41; Robert Embley, Submarine Ring of Fire
_____ __tock, pp. 10, 12, 14; U.S. Geological Survey, p. 102; USGS/Cascades

_____ __/Photo Researchers, Inc.

_____ _gist wearing a special suit designed to protect researchers from heat watches
_____ __na.

Contents

CHAPTER 1

Windows into the Earth

In the spring of 1980, Mount St. Helens began to stir. The beautiful and often-climbed **volcano** in Washington's Cascade Range had been quiet for over a century. After days of earthquakes that gradually became stronger, a volcanic explosion blasted a 250-foot-wide **crater** near the top of the peak. Mount St. Helens had awakened.

...in the next few weeks, the rumbles ...d the crater grew. A bulge appeared on the north side of the volcano as molten rock, or **magma**, rose up from deep within the earth. Scientists monitoring the volcano were very concerned. They knew that if the volcano erupted, it would put many people in danger. Scientists declared a "red zone" in an area around the volcano. Only scientists, law enforcement, and other officials were allowed in this area. Everyone else was ordered to leave and stay outside the red zone. Journalists and tourists joined the group at the edge of the red zone. They hoped to witness the first volcanic eruption in the continental United States since 1914.

May 18, 1980, dawned bright and clear. Dave Johnston, a volcanologist working for the United States Geological Survey, was on duty at an observation post about six miles north of the volcano. Johnston was in charge of studying the gases coming from the volcano. He had studied active volcanoes in Alaska, and understood just how dangerous they could be. Still, he knew that thousands of lives would be at risk when the volcano blew. Someone had to monitor the volcano, so he chose a spot that seemed fairly safe.

At 8:32 A.M., an earthquake shook the volcano. The bulge on the side of Mount St. Helens collapsed and slid away in the largest landslide ever recorded. By radio, Johnston sent the message, "Vancouver! Vancouver! This is it!"[1]

Seconds later, the scientist was engulfed in the gigantic blast, which traveled 17 miles north of the volcano at speeds of up to 300 miles per hour. The blast produced a column of **ash** and **volcanic gas** that rose more than 15 miles into the atmosphere. Over the course of the day, the wind blew 520 million tons of ash eastward, blocking light from the sun. The city of Spokane, 250 miles from the volcano, was plunged into darkness.

Just after noon, avalanches of hot ash, **pumice**, and gas poured out of the crater at 50 to 80 miles per hour. The hot rocks and gas melted some of the snow and ice on top of the volcano, creating a flood of water that mixed with loose rocks and dirt to form a volcanic mudflow, or **lahar**. The lahar poured down the volcano into river valleys, ripping trees from their roots and destroying roads and bridges. In the end, the volcano blast and its aftereffects killed fifty-seven ple, including Johnston. His body was never untless animals died. The surrounding became a wasteland of mud, ash,

cientist

LLAO AND SKELL'S BATTLE: THE MYTH OF CRATER LAKE

Wherever people have lived near active volcanoes, they have invented stories and myths to explain the violent shaking of the earth and the roaring fury of an eruption. Often, these stories carry the seeds of scientific truth. The Klamath people are believed to have witnessed the huge volcanic eruption that formed Crater Lake in Oregon nearly seven thousand years ago. They tell the story of a mighty battle between Llao, the chief of the Below World, and Skell, chief of the Above World. Llao and Skell hurled gigantic stones and fire at each other until finally the ground around Llao collapsed. Llao fell back into the underground world, leaving a huge hole that filled with rain. In fact, scientists now know that there was a huge explosive eruption of the volcano Mount Mazama. The explosion caused the area to collapse, creating a huge sunken pit, or **caldera**. Over time, the caldera filled with water, and Crater Lake was formed. It is the deepest lake in the United States.[3]

A scientist collects information from a Global Positioning System (GPS) station near Mount St. Helens, seen in the distance.

The Mount St. Helens eruption, as terrible as it was, is far from history's most disastrous. The A.D. 79 eruption of Vesuvius, in southern Italy, killed thousands of people living in Pompeii and Herculaneum. In modern times, the 1902 eruption of Mount Pelée in the West Indies completely ⌐oyed the nearby city of St. Pierre and caused the ⌐9,000 people.[4] And in 1985, in the middle ⌐00 people perished when a mudflow

THE YEAR WITHOUT A SUMMER

Volcano disasters are not limited to the immediate area around the eruption. In 1815, Tambora, a volcano on an Indonesian island, erupted. It spewed out an enormous cloud of ash, pumice, and gas. The eruption killed more than ninety thousand people in the immediate area, but its effects were much more far-reaching.

Four hundred million tons of gas reacted with water in the atmosphere, forming tiny droplets of acid that became suspended in the upper part of the atmosphere. The droplets acted like a mirror. They bounced some of the sun's warming rays back into space. It caused the entire planet to get cooler. The year 1816 became known as the Year Without a Summer. All over the Northern Hemisphere, crops failed. There was widespread famine. Hundreds of thousands of people died of hunger or from diseases their bodies were too weak to resist. Other eruptions have caused global cooling, although we know of none as devastating as that of Tambora.[5]

caused by the eruption of the Colombian volcano Nevado del Ruíz engulfed their town.[6]

The Kinder Side of Volcanoes

Volcanoes are not all bad! Over the long term, volcanoes have played a key role in forming and modifying the earth. More than 80 percent of the earth's surface arose from volcanic activity.[7] A few billion years ago, volcanic **vents** spewed out huge amounts

Many people live and grow crops in the shadow of a volcano. Volcanic minerals break down to create fertile soil. These women work near Mount Merapi, a volcano on the Indonesian island of Java.

of water vapor, carbon dioxide, and other gases that helped form the planet's primitive atmosphere. Much of that water condensed and helped form the oceans.[8]

Over time, volcanic materials break down to create rich, fertile soil. This is one of the key reasons that so many people live in the shadow of volcanoes, especially in tropical areas where valuable nutrients in the soils are quickly used up. Most of the large sugar, coffee, and cotton plantations in Central and South America, Indonesia, and the Philippines are located downwind from recently active volcanoes.[9] In many parts of the world, especially in Iceland, people harness the heat generated inside some types of volcanic systems to produce electrical energy. And for scientists, volcanoes offer a fascinating glimpse into Earth's fiery interior.

CHAPTER 2

What Are Volcanoes and Why Do They Erupt?

A volcano is an opening in the earth's surface through which magma emerges. Most people think of volcanoes as majestic, cone-shaped mountains that erupt in great explosions, but volcanoes come in several shapes and sizes. Not all of them erupt explosively. To understand why this is so, it helps to look inside the earth.

In 1864, Jules Verne published what would become a classic science fiction book, *Journey to the Center of the Earth*. In it, a professor and his nephew travel down an extinct volcano in Iceland to the center of the earth. Along the way, they encounter prehistoric plants and animals and have many adventures. At last, they emerge from a volcano in southern Italy.

It is an entertaining story, but a true journey to the center of the earth would be quite different. You would start on the earth's outer layer, or **crust**. Like an eggshell, the crust is brittle and, compared with the layers below, thin. Beneath the oceans, the crust is only about 5 kilometers (3 miles) thick. It is thicker under the continents, averaging about 31 kilometers (19 miles) in depth.

Beneath the earth's crust, you would encounter the **mantle**, a dense, hot layer of semisolid rock. If you could brave the intense pressure and heat, you would travel another 2,900 kilometers (1,800 miles) before you reached the core at the earth's center. The core, which is made mostly of iron and nickel, is very hot: 7,200°C (13,000°F). Verne's professor and his nephew would have to be superhuman to survive that trip!

The upper part of the mantle is cooler and less dense than the deeper mantle. Together with the

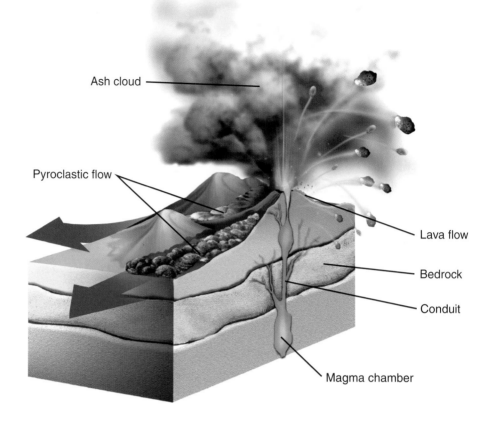

Ash cloud

Pyroclastic flow

Lava flow

Bedrock

Conduit

Magma chamber

The inside of a volcano

crust, it forms a thick layer of huge rock slabs called tectonic plates. According to **plate tectonics**, these plates float atop the earth's mantle, moving in response to forces deep within the earth. As the mantle rises closer to the surface, it becomes liquid, or molten. This molten rock, mixed with dissolved gases and crystals, is magma.

As the magma rises, some of it collects in pools, sometimes called **magma chambers**. Volcanoes occur when magma breaks through the crust or pushes up between two plates. Once the magma has erupted from a volcano, it is called **lava**.

About two-thirds of the earth's volcanoes lie along ridges under the ocean where two tectonic plates are slowly separating. Magma rises through the vents, creating new crust under the ocean. Because these underwater volcanoes are hidden from ordinary view, we do not know as much about them as the more familiar land-based volcanoes. Underwater volcanoes are an exciting new area of research for volcanologists.

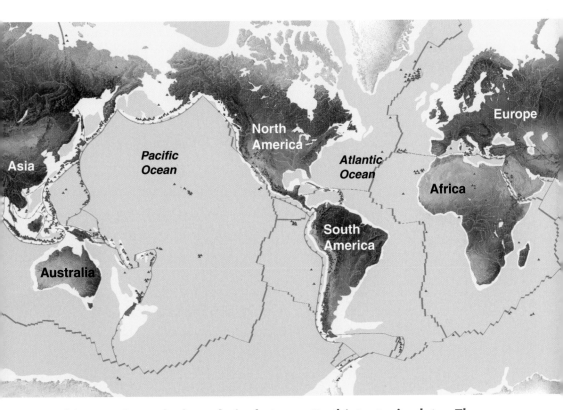

This map shows the boundaries between Earth's tectonic plates. The red dots are locations of volcanoes. The many volcanoes near the Pacific Ocean are called the Ring of Fire.

WHY ARE SOME ERUPTIONS MORE DANGEROUS THAN OTHERS?

Mount St. Helens erupted in a violent explosion. The eruptions on Kilauea, in Hawaii, are usually so safe that they are a major tourist attraction. What is the difference? The danger depends on the amount of dissolved gas and **silica**, the main component of most types of sand, in the magma. It also depends on how fast the magma rises. The more silica in the magma, the more gooey, or viscous, it will be. If the magma is very sticky, like tar, the gases cannot escape easily. Pressure builds until the lava and gas, along with dust, ashes, and solid rocks, escape in a violent explosion. This was what happened with the Mount St. Helens eruption.

If the magma is low in silica, it is very fluid, like warm molasses. The gases can escape easily, and the eruption will be fairly quiet. Kilauea's magma is low in silica. The lava tends to flow, rather than explode, from the volcano.

Other volcanoes occur when two plates collide or grind against one another. One plate is pushed beneath a second plate in areas called **subduction zones**. The sinking plate partially melts to form magma. Because it is lighter, the magma rises and can erupt through the upper plate as a volcano.

Some volcanoes, such as those on the Hawaiian Islands or the one under Yellowstone National Park, are located in the middle of a plate. They are said to be above **hot spots**, which act like blowtorches thrusting up from the mantle.

Volcanoes Come in Different Shapes and Sizes

Repeated eruptions build volcanoes of different shapes, depending on the type of magma within. Here are some of the basic types of volcanoes.

Shield volcanoes are so named because they are shaped like an ancient warrior's shield. They are broad, shallow-sided mounds topped by large, flat-bottomed craters. Kilauea is an example of a shield volcano. Its low-silica magma produces long, fluid lava flows that puddle on land or flow into the sea. Over time, the lava builds up, creating a gently sloping mound. Shield volcanoes are also often found on the **ocean crust**.

The smallest volcanoes, **cinder cones**, are formed by runny low-silica magma that still contains a lot of dissolved gas. These volcanoes tend to explode and sputter like soda spraying from a shaken can. The erupting lava breaks apart into fragments called cinders. These cinders settle around the vent in a conical shape. Sunset Crater in Arizona is an example of a cinder cone. These volcanoes sometimes form on the flanks of larger volcanoes.

Some of the world's most famous (or infamous) volcanoes are **stratovolcanoes**. Italy's Vesuvius, Washington's Mount St. Helens, and Japan's Mount Fuji are all stratovolcanoes. They contain viscous magma. Most of these volcanoes begin erupting with an explosion of ash and cinders, followed by flows of lava. This is why they are sometimes called composite volcanoes. The layering of ash and lava forms their steep slopes. Stratovolcanoes are often found along subduction zones.

On the outer slopes of many stratovolcanoes, or even within their summit craters, are smaller volcanoes called lava domes. They are made by thick, slow-moving lava that squeezes out of the earth, much like toothpaste from its tube. In 2008, there was a new lava dome erupting in Mount St. Helens.[1]

Very gooey, high-silica magma can accumulate for a long time in huge underground chambers. When the magma finally erupts, it does so quickly. The unsupported roof of rock above the chamber collapses. This creates large craters with steep walls. These craters are called calderas. Yellowstone National Park sits on a caldera that is 80 kilometers (50 miles) long and 56 kilometers (35 miles) wide. A giant explosion created it six hundred forty thousand years ago.[2]

CHAPTER 3

Lessons from a Bronze Age Pompeii

The plain of Campania is in southern Italy. It has wonderfully fertile soil, beautiful weather, and access to the Mediterranean Sea. To the people who lived there nearly four thousand years ago, it must have seemed an ideal place to grow crops and raise livestock. Ideal, that is, until the nearby mountain that we now call Vesuvius blew its top.

The Bronze Age villagers living near the modern-day city of Nola must have been taken by surprise when Vesuvius exploded. The volcano, nine miles away, erupted with a mighty boom. It sent a cloud of superheated dust and ash 35 kilometers (22 miles) into the air. Volcanic rocks rained from the sky. A wave of hot ash, dust, and gas raced down the slopes of the volcano at up to 240 kilometers (150 miles) per hour. This **pyroclastic surge** destroyed everything in its path. The villagers fled, leaving a dog and nine pregnant goats in a pen. Perhaps they hoped to find these valuable animals safe when they returned.

When the villagers came back, they found their homes, their animals, and their fields buried under about 4.6 meters (15 feet) of ash and mud. Some people tried to create a new village, but it was soon abandoned. The ash-covered desert was not yet ready to sustain their farming way of life. Over time, the plain of Campania recovered. People built new villages and cities. It would be over two thousand years before Vesuvius destroyed another, much more famous settlement: Pompeii (see sidebar).

Lessons from the Past

Giuseppe Mastrolorenzo and Lucia Pappalardo, volcanologists at the Vesuvius Observatory in Naples,

POMPEII

As far as the residents of Pompeii and neighboring towns were concerned, the morning of August 24, A.D. 79, was much like any other. To be sure, there had been a few small tremors of the earth, but these small earthquakes were fairly common in the region. They might have noticed a small cloud rising from Mount Vesuvius a few miles away, but most people continued with their daily business throughout the morning. Most of them were not even aware that Vesuvius was a volcano; it had been quiet for hundreds of years.

At one o'clock that afternoon, Vesuvius awoke with a mighty explosion. Roman writer Pliny the Younger witnessed the eruption from his vantage point across the Bay of Naples, 32 kilometers (20 miles) from Vesuvius. Years later, Pliny described the eruption cloud that arose from the volcano as being shaped like a pine tree, rising into the sky on a very long trunk with branches spreading out. (Scientists now call these kinds of extremely violent eruptions *Plinian*.)

Within minutes, the cloud had risen over ten miles high. Soon, ash, pumice, and larger volcanic rocks began to rain down upon Pompeii. People took shelter as fist-sized rocks crashed to the ground, but then roofs collapsed under the weight of the debris. Many people tried to flee, pillows tied to their heads to protect themselves from the falling rocks.

At about one o'clock the next morning, the eruption entered an even more dangerous phase. As the eruption weakened, the gigantic cloud began to collapse in six separate waves. Each wave produced a **pyroclastic flow** of superheated gas and rock fragments, followed by a surge of gas and ash that moved as fast as 100 kilometers (60 miles) per hour. The hot ash clouds flattened walls and suffocated those who had not managed to escape earlier.

By the time the eruption ended, 3.7 meters (12 feet) of volcanic debris covered Pompeii. Herculaneum, a seaside resort nearby, was buried under 23 meters (76 feet) of ash from the pyroclastic flows and surges.

The cities, and the remains of the victims, were hidden for hundreds of years. People digging for art objects in the eighteenth century discovered them. Over the years, archaeologists have worked to excavate Pompeii and Herculaneum. Visitors can wander the streets of the once-buried cities, where houses, shops, public baths, theaters, and temples are on display.

There have been much more destructive volcanic eruptions since the one that destroyed Pompeii and Herculaneum. Still, the A.D. 79 eruption of Vesuvius is one of the most infamous examples of a volcano's fury.

Italy, have been working with American volcanologist Michael Sheridan and Italian anthropologist Pier Paolo Petrone to piece together the story of what happened in the Bronze Age catastrophe.[1] What they have learned has the scientists worried.

Until recently, scientists believed that the volcano's worst eruption was the notorious one that buried Pompeii in A.D. 79. In 1993, however, Mastrolorenzo and other scientists uncovered evidence that the Bronze Age eruption, now known as the Avellino eruption, was much more destructive.

If a similar eruption were to occur today,

Mount Vesuvius destroyed the city of Pompeii in A.D. 79.

Mastrolorenzo and Pappalardo say that the 3 million people who live in and around Naples would be at risk of the same fate as those Bronze Age people. But escaping the crowded region would be much more difficult today.

"I had many friends who were archaeologists and were interested in studying the Bronze Age civilization in the Campanian plain," Mastrolorenzo explained. In 1995, the archaeologists were digging a test hole for a pipeline that was to be laid about ten miles northeast of Vesuvius. They found two skeletons, a male and a female, buried under ancient volcanic material. "My friends called me in the night, and said, 'Pepe [Giuseppe], there is a very interesting **excavation**. You must come see it!'"[2]

Working with Petrone, Mastrolorenzo found that the victims died of suffocation and had been very quickly buried under about three feet of **lapilli**— pumice fragments up to 6.4 centimeters (2.5 inches) in diameter. "We knew that there must have been a village nearby, because it is very hard to walk on this pumice lapilli," Mastrolorenzo said.

Sure enough, in 2001, Mastrolorenzo got another call from some archaeologists. Construction workers digging a foundation for a new grocery store on the

Volcanologist Lucia Pappalardo monitors the temperature of gas at fumaroles in Solfatara crater near Naples, Italy, by using an infrared thermal camera.

outskirts of the town of Nola had uncovered traces of charred wood a few feet below the surface, along with volcanic rocks. Over the next few months, the archaeologists unearthed three large horseshoe-shaped huts with many pots, pottery plates, and jars holding grain, flour, and other kinds of food. "It is probably the best preserved Bronze Age village in the world," Mastrolorenzo said. Like Pompeii, it has been frozen in time.

A few years later, archaeologists discovered thousands of human and animal footprints deposits headed away from the volcano in Avellino. This was just four miles outside of present-day Naples.

Like detectives solving a mystery, Mastrolorenzo and Pappalardo use the clues left in the deposits to reconstruct what happened on that terrifying day nearly four thousand years ago. The eruption column collapsed in a series of pyroclastic surges and flows, creating searing hot avalanches of ash and gas that raced down the slopes of the volcano. It covered the entire countryside around Vesuvius with a thick layer of ash. The surges and flows reached well into the present-day metropolitan area of Naples, covering that region with up to three meters (ten feet) of deposits. Computer models show that they moved with a force strong enough to blast down many modern buildings.

Finally, heavy rains triggered by the eruption created great mudflows, or lahars, that covered everything with a blanket of dirt and ash. "Imagine what it was like to return," Mastrolorenzo said. "It had to be terrifying."

Planning for the Future

"If an eruption like Avellino occurs again, the scenario will be the same," said Pappalardo, who is from a city near Naples. "The whole area, including my mother city, will become a desert again. Where will those three million people go, and how long will they have to wait until they can return?"[3]

Many local people, especially the older generation, do not share the scientists' worries. Some remember the last eruption in 1944, which was relatively small. Although one town was partially destroyed, people were able to get out of harm's way, and there were few casualties. They think that the next eruption will be much like that one. The official evacuation plan is based on a Pompeii-like eruption as the worst-case scenario. The plan assumes that 600,000 people in the towns and villages surrounding Vesuvius will need to be evacuated—but not the residents of Naples. Mastrolorenzo and Pappalardo think this is a mistake. An eruption similar to the one that destroyed the Bronze Age village would threaten Naples as well.

Scientists know from studying the geologic records that Vesuvius has unleashed catastrophic eruptions roughly every two thousand years. Scientists calculate that there is more than a 50 percent chance that Vesuvius will erupt violently in the next few years.[4]

There are other signs that Vesuvius may be preparing for "the big one." By examining the chemistry of

Volcanologist Guiseppe Mastrolorenzo examines volcanic rock near Vesuvius.

the rocks from the Avellino eruption, scientists found that the magma had been rich with gas. They could also tell that the magma came from a chamber five miles under Vesuvius. These are the conditions we see today, Pappalardo said. By contrast, the magma in the 1944 eruption was less rich in gas, and came from a deeper chamber.

Modern techniques of monitoring volcanic activity ensure that people living near Vesuvius will not be completely taken by surprise when the volcano erupts again. But how much advance notice will they have? And how severe will the next eruption be?

"We don't know," said Mastrolorenzo. "We will see signs of an eruption coming weeks, maybe even years, in advance. We will see swarms of small earthquakes. The ground surrounding the volcano will push upward. There will be changes in the composition and the volume of the gas in the magma. At that time we will be very close to the time of the eruption."

Pappalardo and Mastrolorenzo recently completed a laboratory experiment showing that the more explosive the eruption, the less time it takes for the magma to rise to the surface. The buildup phase of a very large eruption, Pappalardo said, might last for

VULCAN'S FORGE

In the Tyrrhenian Sea, just off the island of Sicily, lies a small island called Vulcano. The ancient Romans believed that the island was the chimney of the forge of Vulcan, a blacksmith and the god of fire. Fire and smoke belched from the chimney as Vulcan hammered out thunderbolts for Jupiter, king of the gods, and weapons for Mars, the god of war. This small volcanic island gave us the English word for volcano.[5]

years, even centuries, but the final phase happens very quickly.

Scientists, then, will have a pretty good idea of when the volcano will erupt, but it is very difficult to tell how big the explosion will be—at least, not very far in advance. Nobody wants to be like the boy who cried wolf at the first sign of an eruption, calling for a major evacuation of the region if Vesuvius decides just to "burp." On the other hand, given the legendary traffic snarls in and around Naples, nobody wants to wait until the last minute to get people to safety.

For Mastrolorenzo and Pappalardo, there is no question that Vesuvius will have another violent eruption similar to the Pompeii and Avellino eruptions. They do not know whether it will happen in their lifetimes, but if it does, their research will no doubt give people a better idea of what to expect.

The Making of a Volcanologist

Pappalardo's interest in volcanoes comes naturally. "I was born in a little town at the base of Vesuvius, Torre del Greco," she said. Much of the city was destroyed by an eruption in 1631, and also suffered damage in later, less severe eruptions. Each time, the people of Torre del Greco rebuilt and repaired their city on the same spot. As a child, she believed that "if we knew how Vesuvius works, we could save a lot of lives. Not the town, because we know that it will be destroyed again. But we can save the people."

Mastrolorenzo had a more roundabout interest in **volcanology**. "When I was a child, I was not much interested in volcanoes," he said. "I was most interested in astronomy, in the origin of rocks and the planets. I realized that the most easy-to-study planet is Earth, and the best way to study the origin of rocks is to study volcanology." Because volcanic rocks are newly formed from the interior of the planet, he explained, they can tell us a lot about the ways in which planets are formed.

CHAPTER 4

At Home with Pele

Native Hawaiians told the story of how the beautiful volcano goddess Pele ran away from her parents and jealous sister. She crossed the ocean and landed on a coral reef near Kauai. There, she used her digging stick to create a fire pit. Not quite satisfied, she moved southeastward, first to the island of Oahu, then to Molokai, Maui, and finally to the Big Island of Hawaii. There, she dug her last fire pit on the floor of Kilauea, one of the most active volcanoes in the world today.[1]

Volcanologist Jim Kauahikaua

The Science Behind the Myths

As a native of Hawaii, volcanologist Jim Kauahikaua grew up learning about Pele. Kauahikaua, scientist-in-charge at the Hawaiian Volcano Observatory, said that understanding the local mythology is a big plus when it comes to the volcano hazards field.

"One of the reasons that people told these stories was to pass on information about local hazards," Kauahikaua said. "They declared that the summit area [of a volcano] was sacred. They were trying to pass on information so that future generations could avoid the really dire effects of volcano hazards."[2]

As a boy, Kauahikaua was interested in science and the outdoors. Surrounded by water, a career in oceanography seemed like a natural choice for him. When he went to college, he took a geology course his first semester. He liked it so much that he switched his major immediately, earning a bachelor's degree in geology from Pomona College in California. "Coming from Hawaii, it was a natural path to volcanoes," Kauahikaua said. He returned to the islands to earn a master of science degree and, later, a doctorate, both in geophysics, at the University of Hawaii.

The Pele myth indicates that the ancient Hawaiians were keen observers of their home. The islands actually were created by volcanic eruptions at the bottom of the ocean. Over millions of years, lava from the eruptions continued to build up. When the lava broke through the surface of the ocean, a new island was born. In fact, there is a baby island being formed by underwater eruptions at the southeastern end of the chain. Scientists estimate that it will surface in about fifty thousand years.

Just as Pele traveled from one island to the next in search of the perfect home, modern geologists confirm that the volcanoes on Kauai—the northwest island of the chain—are older than those on the southeastern end. That is because the Pacific tectonic plate is passing over a hot spot in the mantle at a rate of about four inches per year.[3] The plate acts somewhat like a conveyer belt, pulling existing volcanoes away from the hot spot. As they leave the hot spot, they become extinct.

A Long-lasting Eruption

Kilauea, on the Big Island of Hawaii, has been erupting steadily since 1983. This would be disastrous if its eruptions were explosive, but Hawaiian volcanic eruptions tend to be relatively gentle. This makes Kilauea a popular place for scientists and tourists alike to visit.

Although most mainland volcanoes erupt from a crater in the center, Hawaiian volcanoes can erupt from cracks, called rift zones, extending from the summit. The magma pushes up into the summit crater, and then moves along the rift zones where it can erupt. Since 1983, lava has poured from a crater called Pu'u 'O'o (POO oo OH oh) along Kilauea's eastern side. (*Pu'u* is the Hawaiian word for hill, and *'O'o* is the name for Pele's digging stick.[4])

Sometimes, the lava flow is covered with cooled fragments or rubble. This is called **'a'a** lava—burning or glowing lava—and it can move down channels as quickly as a fast runner. At other times, the lava flow has a smooth, shiny skin that ripples and flows. This is called **pahoehoe** lava. It moves more slowly, through tubes formed when the outer surface of the flow crusts over. In any case, the lava flows can advance for miles, often emptying into the ocean. The Hawaiians say that the ocean is the home of Namakaokahai, Pele's jealous sister. When Pele's hot lava meets Namakaokahai's cool water, they meet much like two angry sisters—with lots of sizzle and sometimes even explosions.

People can easily get out of the way of advancing lava flows, but buildings, roads, and plants are not so fortunate. While Kilauea's eruptions have caused few deaths since the 1800s, lava flows have covered or destroyed entire towns, forests, and parkland. Hawaiians tend to take the loss of property in stride. "To live on an active volcano and not accept the possibility of the volcano somehow affecting you, either by earthquakes, lava flows, or gas emissions, would be foolhardy," Kauahikaua said.

Kauahikaua studies the formation of **lava tubes** and the movement of lava flows. His research helps scientists estimate the path of the next lava flow and what it might threaten. Kauahikaua is also interested in learning more about what is inside a volcano. He cannot tunnel into a volcano, of course, but he has other ways of "looking" inside. For example, he can measure how well different parts of the volcano conduct electricity. Dry rock, especially on an active volcano, does not conduct electricity very well. But water—especially salty ocean water—is a good conductor of electricity. "On islands, at least in the coastal areas, there's an invasion of seawater that seeps into the underlying rock," Kauahikaua said. Freshwater from rainfall seeps into the rock, too. Magma is also a good conductor of electricity. By using instruments that measure how well different

Fountaining and lava flow from Pu'u 'O'o at Hawaii Volcanoes National Park

This scientist is sampling 'a'a lava at Kilauea.

areas conduct electricity, he can figure out what is inside the volcano—and where.

It is important to know where there might be hidden pockets of water, because they can affect eruptions. If water comes into contact with hot rock or magma, it can flash into steam. If the steam becomes trapped, the pressure builds until it escapes in a violent explosion. In 1924, steam explosions from

Kilauea blew mud, debris, and hot rocks as far as two-thirds of a mile from the crater. Columns of ash and dust rose more than two miles into the air. An even more explosive eruption took place in 1790. A group of warriors and their families were taken by surprise

This geologist takes measurements from a lava tube window at Kilauea.

THE WORLD'S LARGEST VOLCANO

Mauna Loa, also on the Big Island of Hawaii, is another of the world's most active volcanoes. It has erupted 33 times since 1842. Although it has not erupted since 1984, scientists are certain that it will do so again.

Mauna Loa is the world's largest active volcano as well as the largest mountain. It rises to more than 4 kilometers (2.5 miles) above sea level, but its base is on the ocean floor some 5 kilometers (3 miles) below the surface. It is so heavy that the Pacific tectonic plate upon which it rests sags 8 kilometers (5 miles) under its weight![5]

Mauna Loa may well be the most dangerous volcano in Hawaii. It can send out very long lava flows. The city of Hilo lies directly in the path of one of the lava flows. Over the centuries, people have tried different ways to protect their

when Kilauea exploded. At least 80 people—maybe more—were killed in that deadly eruption.[6]

A Father's Day Surprise

Since Kauahikaua was named scientist-in-charge at the Hawaiian Volcano Observatory in 2004, he has not had as much time to pursue his own research. He visits the area often, usually in a helicopter, writes regular updates about the volcano's activity, and property from destruction, including making offerings to Pele. In a 1935 eruption, a river of lava began to move slowly down the valley toward Hilo. It looked as though it might destroy the city. The director of the Hawaiian Volcano Observatory, Thomas Jagger, had an idea. He asked the U.S. Army Air Corps to send in airplanes to attack the advancing flow with bombs. The flow did stop short of Hilo, although scientists now believe that the lava flow had stopped because the eruption had ended—not because of the bombs.

Mauna Loa erupted again in 1942, during World War II. Already at war with Japan, the U.S. Army Air Corps was called in once more to wage war with the lava flow. The bombs only succeeded in creating a new flow near the old one. The lava flow stopped before reaching Hilo, but it probably was not due to the bombing. Hilo has been threatened by lava flows since then, but the government decided that it would no longer try to change their courses.[7]

generally oversees day-to-day operations of the observatory.

On June 17, 2007, Father's Day, Pele sprang a surprise. Until that day, the Pu'u 'O'o crater had been fairly predictable: When it erupted, the lava flowed down a tube all the way to the coast. It followed a path that had been covered by lava deposits for years. It did not pose any hazards, and in fact it was a fairly large tourist attraction, Kauahikaua said. Early that morning, the observatory's monitors picked up a swarm of small earthquakes. Over the next few days, the scientists noticed more earthquake swarms, and new cracks and eruption sites formed along the rift. Pu'u 'O'o's lava flow stopped for a couple of weeks, its magma supply shut off.

Then, on July 21, 2007, just as Harry Potter fans got their hands on the last book of J.K. Rowling's series, Pele again demonstrated some of her power. Pu'u 'O'o erupted again, but this time the lava flowed in a different direction. Kauahikaua is carefully studying this new lava flow to determine whether it might pose a threat to communities in its path. From a scientific standpoint, this newest eruption at the Pu'u 'O'o vent is a gold mine. "We have an amazing record of the eruption so far," Kauahikaua said. "It's probably the best documented episode ever—of any volcano in the world. Once the hazard issue dies down and we're actually able to study this eruption, there will be an amazing data set." This will give scientists a new look at the plumbing of the Pu'u 'O'o chamber.

Working so closely to an erupting volcano can lead to some memorable experiences. In 1996, scientists monitoring Kilauea noted a large number of small earthquakes at the summit. The eruption they thought would come next never happened. Instead, the volcano sent a very large pulse of magma to the Pu'u 'O'o crater. Kauahikaua flew over the crater in a helicopter to see what was going on. Before this, he said, the lava had been flowing through a fairly large tube system down to the ocean. After this pulse, the system could not handle the amount of lava coming through. Lava began gushing from a hole in the tube, shooting six to nine meters (twenty to thirty feet) into the air.

Kauahikaua happened to have a monitoring location set up on the lava tube just above the hole. "I had a real opportunity to measure this pulse of lava coming out," he said. "That meant I had to work within 100 feet [30 meters] or so of lava gushing out of a hole in the tube." Standing on the tube as the lava inside rushed under his feet, Kauahikaua made his measurements. He was not frightened because he was familiar with the volcano. "But it was definitely a very dramatic moment."

Volcanoes Are Out of This World!

Rosaly Lopes is listed in *The Guinness Book of World Records* for discovering more active volcanoes than anyone else in history. As of 2007, she had discovered 71. But Lopes, a geologist and volcanologist at NASA's Jet Propulsion Laboratory (JPL) in California, has not visited a single one of them. She discovered the volcanoes on Io, one of the moons of the planet Jupiter. She did it with the help of an instrument on board the spacecraft *Galileo*, named in honor of the famous Italian astronomer.

Io: A Hot Spot for Volcanoes

Lopes first heard that Io had active volcanoes on a cold, gray day in England when the news of anything hot, even on another planet, was good news.[1] The year was 1979, and the Brazilian woman, who was born and raised in sunny Rio de Janeiro, was working on her Ph.D. at the University of London Observatory. *Voyager 1*, one of two pioneering spacecraft launched in 1977 to explore the planets, had sent pictures of Io back to scientists on Earth. The scientists had dubbed Io the "pizza moon" because its many large craters made it look like a pepperoni pizza. The pictures revealed mixtures of particles and gas, or **plumes**, shooting far from the surface of the moon. A heat-detecting instrument on board the spacecraft showed that the plumes were very hot. Io definitely had active volcanoes!

This was exciting, because before that time, most scientists thought that the only active volcanoes in the solar system were on Earth. Lopes would continue to

Rosaly Lopes has studied volcanoes on Earth—and in space!

study volcanoes on Earth and Mars for her Ph.D., but that image of Io stuck with her. "I daydreamed about what it would be like to work on a flight project like *Voyager*, to be part of a team that saw images from other worlds before anybody else. Io had set my course."[2]

When she started work at JPL in 1989, Lopes joined a scientific team responsible for an instrument on the spacecraft *Galileo*, which had just been launched. Its mission was to investigate Jupiter and its moons. As it orbited Jupiter thirty-four times, instruments on board the spacecraft took pictures and gathered data, sending it all back to the scientists on Earth. Guided by the scientists, *Galileo* measured Jupiter's atmosphere, found evidence of an ocean under the surface of three of its moons, and revealed the volcanic activity on Io.

Lopes and her colleagues used an instrument that measured both reflected sunlight and heat to look for volcanoes on Io. The early observations, Lopes said, were made far away from the moon, which is surrounded by very intense radiation. They knew that the radiation could severely damage the spacecraft and its instruments. But if they wanted to learn more about the volcanoes, *Galileo* had to fly closer to Io. Near the end of the mission, the scientists and engineers decided to take a chance. They agreed to send *Galileo* in for some closer flybys.

The spacecraft survived, although some of the instruments were damaged by the radiation. Even so, the data they gathered was "rich and full of surprises," according to Lopes. "Io was much more volcanically active than we had realized from the distant observations. The closer we got, the more hot spots we could detect." She and her colleagues eventually detected 166 hot spots, or active volcanoes.

She estimated that she personally detected 71 of them. Detecting hot spots on Io may not be a major scientific finding, she wrote, but it was "certainly fun."[3]

The volcanoes are much hotter and erupt more frequently than Earth's volcanoes today. One of Io's volcanoes, Loki, is more powerful than all of Earth's volcanoes combined. This is why scientists say that Io is the most volcanic body in the solar system, even though Earth actually has more active volcanoes. Scientists believe that the volcanic activity on Io may be very similar to the activity that occurred on Earth when it was a very young planet. This makes Io an ideal laboratory for learning about what Earth may have been like more than 4 billion years ago.

Lopes said that volcanic activity on Io is not related to plate tectonics, as it is on Earth. Instead, Io is like the rope in a kind of tug-of-war between Jupiter and two of Jupiter's other large moons, Ganymede and Europa. On Earth, we have ocean tides because the Moon's gravity pulls a bit harder on the side closer to the Moon than the other side. The tug-of-war causes tides on Io, too, but they are tides in the moon's crust itself! This causes heat to build up inside the moon, resulting in lots of volcanic activity.

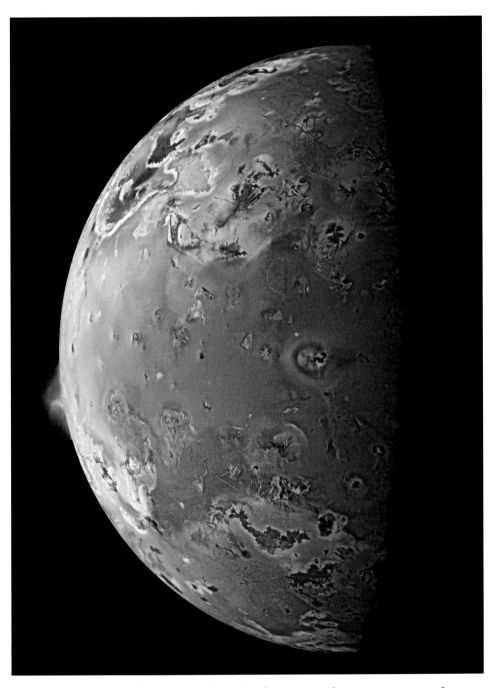

In this picture of Io, two volcanic plumes can be seen, one on the moon's left edge and another in the center. Plumes on Io have a blue color with a red shadow.

The *Galileo* mission is over, but Lopes continues to study the data sent back from the spacecraft, even as she has turned her attention to a very different place in the solar system.

Ice Volcanoes on Titan

In 2002, Lopes became part of a team of scientists working on the *Cassini* mission to Saturn, and its moons and rings. The *Cassini* spacecraft, launched in 1997, finally entered Saturn's orbit in 2004. By 2008, Lopes and others were studying and mapping the surface of Titan, Saturn's largest moon. (Saturn has dozens of moons.) Titan's surface lies under a blanket of orange haze—mostly nitrogen and methane gases.

THE MAN IN THE MOON

Have you ever wondered about the Man in the Moon? Ancient astronomers called the dark areas on Earth's Moon that form the Man's features *lunar maria* (from the Latin for "moon seas"), because they looked like oceans. In fact, those dark areas are actually plains of lava. They are a result of volcanic activity that took place billions of years ago.

VOLCANOES ON MARS

While there has never been a man on Mars, real or imagined, there is a possibility that life of some sort may have once existed there. There is strong evidence that there used to be oceans on Mars. Where there is liquid water, there may be life.

Although the surface of the Red Planet is very cold now (−46°C, or −51°F), scientists have suggested that ancient volcanic activity may have once warmed Mars enough for liquid water oceans to form.[4] Mars has many extinct volcanoes, including a giant shield volcano, Olympus Mons. Three times as tall as Mount Everest and as wide as the entire chain of Hawaiian Islands, it is the largest volcano in our solar system. Billions of years ago, when the volcanoes on Mars were active, it is likely that they produced large amounts of a sulfur compound. This compound, sulfur dioxide, would have trapped heat from the sun, making Mars warm enough to support life. When the Martian volcanoes went extinct and stopped producing sulfur dioxide, scientists say, the planet would have become too cold to support life.

Scientists are keenly interested in Titan because it is the only moon in the solar system known to have clouds and a planet-like atmosphere. The conditions on Titan may even resemble those on Earth several billion years ago, before there was oxygen in the atmosphere.

Cassini is equipped with a special radar instrument designed to penetrate Titan's haze. The moon is finally revealing some of its secrets. "Every time we have a new flyby," Lopes said, "we see new ground. Titan was very largely unexplored . . . before *Cassini*."[5]

During the first flyby that returned data, Lopes spotted a volcano. As it turned out, she got lucky—there are not that many volcanoes on Titan, and none of them seem to be active. "If we had found no volcanoes, I would have had to change my specialty or something!" she joked. The one she found was unlike any volcano on Earth. It was a **cryovolcano**—an icy volcano!

Because Titan is so far away from the sun, it is very cold. Its crust is mostly ice. Underneath is water and liquid ammonia. Instead of erupting molten rock, Titan's cryovolcanoes erupt an icy water-ammonia mixture. "Although they seem very different from volcanoes on Earth, cryovolcanoes can make very much the same type of features that you get with lava," Lopes said.

The team found a circular feature, called Ganesa Macula, about 179 kilometers (111 miles) in diameter. It resembles a Hawaiian shield volcano, with

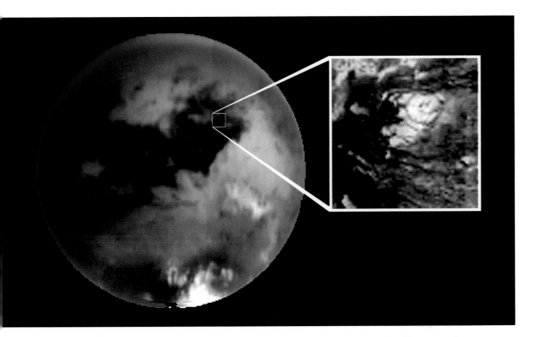

This false-color image of Titan shows what scientists believe to be a cryovolcano (ice volcano). The inset is a higher resolution image of the volcano.

channels—possibly formed by the icy lava—winding down the mountainside from a central crater.

Lopes and her team stitched together radar images from several different Titan flybys to create maps of the surface. They found giant lakes and seas filled with liquid methane and ethane. (On Earth, methane is one of the greenhouse gases that contribute to global warming. Ethane is another common gas on Earth.) Lopes and her colleagues think that volcanic eruptions or erosion may have caused depressions where liquids could collect.

Lopes spends much of her time planning observations. During a flyby, "there is a very limited time when the spacecraft is close enough to make observations," she said. "There are usually dozens of instruments on the spacecraft, and lots of people want to make observations with their instruments as well." The most exciting times for Lopes are when she gets new data from the instruments. "It's really like discovering a new world. You don't know what you're going to find. That's the most exciting part."

Dreams of a Would-be Astronaut

"I wanted to work for NASA [National Aeronautics and Space Administration] since I was a kid," said Lopes. "My earliest memories were of my parents talking about Yuri Gagarin [the first human in space]. I was about three or four, but I remember it very well. Exploring space was my main goal."

As Lopes got older, she realized that she would probably never be an astronaut. At that time, no woman had ever gone into space. She was from Brazil, a country that did not have an active space program. And she was nearsighted. Still looking at the stars, she studied astronomy at the University of London, where she received her bachelor of science degree in 1978. "In my final semester, I took a course in planetary geology and loved it. One day, my professor didn't come to class because he had gone to study the eruption of Mount Etna [in Italy]. That seemed terribly exciting to me."

She decided to combine her interests by studying planetary geology and volcanology in graduate school. "My adviser told me that you can't understand volcanoes on other planets unless you understand them on Earth," she said. "It was kind of funny, because I grew up in Brazil by the sea, and although I did lots of sports related to swimming and the ocean, I was very much a city girl. So when I went to my first volcano, I was a real beginner. I didn't even own a pair of hiking boots. It was quite a new life."

As it turned out, her first volcano experience was truly one to remember. The budding volcanologist was part of a team of scientists surveying Mount Etna, on the Italian island of Sicily. Her job that summer was to study lava flows. She wanted to learn how they were shaped by the ground over which they traveled. (She eventually used these studies to determine how lava on the surface of Mars must have flowed many years ago.) They were just finishing up their work on September 12, 1979, when something unexpected happened: Mount Etna exploded. Built-up gas or steam blew chunks of rock out of the crater at deadly speeds. Rock **bombs** killed nine people; Lopes and her colleagues helped rescue many others. "In one evening, Etna taught me that the work of a volcanologist is not all science and adventure. Our science had failed these people, because we still know so little about how volcanoes work."[6]

Lopes urges would-be scientists to follow their dreams. "Even within planetary science or volcanology, there are many different types of things that you can do." You can do fieldwork, for example, or create models of volcanoes on computers to understand how they work. There is something for everyone in volcanology.

CHAPTER 6

Volcanoes Are a Gas!

Ken Sims grew up hiking and climbing mountains with his dad and his dad's buddies. When he was in the third grade, he climbed to the top of Pikes Peak, Colorado, with his father. Before becoming a volcanologist, Ken was a professional mountaineer and climbing guide. He has climbed Denali

John Catto, Alpenglow Pictures

in Alaska, the highest peak in North America. He has scaled frozen waterfalls, and he has been a mountain guide for scientists in Antarctica. If anybody has the skills and ability to safely lower himself into a smoking crater, it is Sims. But why would he want to lower himself into the mouth of a smoky, smelly, hot, active volcano? Because for Sims, that is where the action is, scientifically speaking.

Sims is a volcanologist at the Woods Hole Oceanographic Institution in Massachusetts. He studies the gas produced by volcanoes, from the mid-ocean ridge in the Atlantic to Mount Erebus in Antarctica. For his research, the closer he can get to the source, the better. He seeks out volcanoes that emit plenty of gas—but are in no danger

John Catto, Alpenglow Pictures

Dr. Ken Sims

of erupting while he is working in the crater. The gas samples he collects help him learn more about the origins and movement of magma in the earth's mantle, and about the "plumbing system" of volcanoes. He also studies the gases of volcanoes on land for signs of a coming eruption—and how they might be used to alert nearby residents.

Telling Time with Rock Clocks

The magma that lies beneath volcanoes contains a variety of gases. When the magma is deep under the surface of the earth, it is under a lot of pressure. Like carbon dioxide gas in a sealed can of soda, these gases are dissolved in the magma. As magma rises to the surface, the surrounding pressure lessens. The drop in pressure allows the dissolved gases to escape the magma, much like the fizz that escapes from a just-opened soda can. If the magma is rising slowly, the gas escapes slowly as well, in "belches" or "burps." These eruptions are effusive. If the magma rises rapidly, the gas escapes suddenly in an explosive eruption.

Volcanic gas typically contains a mixture of chemicals. They include water vapor, radon, carbon dioxide, sulfur dioxide, and hydrogen sulfide—the last two give volcanoes a characteristic rotten-egg smell. Sims is especially interested in radon, a minor ingredient in the gas mix with a major story to tell.

Radon is a colorless, odorless gas that comes from uranium, an element in Earth's crust and mantle. Radon and uranium are **radioactive** elements, which means that their atoms cast off particles of energy we call radiation. In this process, called radioactive decay, the atoms of one element—the parent—change into atoms of a different, or daughter, element. Some radioactive elements take billions of years to decay; others decay in under a second. The amount of time required for half of the atoms of a radioactive element to decay is called the element's half-life. By comparing the ratio of the parent element to the daughter element, scientists can tell how long the radioactive "clock" has been ticking.

Many elements, including radon, come in different forms, called **isotopes**. Radon, for example, has thirty-four isotopes, with half-lives ranging from under a second to several days. "One of the isotopes I study has a half-life of just one minute, so measuring it in my gas sample helps me understand the processes that happened in the past ten minutes in the magma system," Sims said. "If you think of the volcano as having a plumbing system, then you want to understand whether the magma moves really fast from the source all the way to the top. Does it get stuck in the pipes somewhere, and if so, where and for how long? Does it change composition? These are questions that you can't answer without these radon clocks."[1]

Volcanic gases also contain tiny amounts of rare heavy metals. Sims says that these metals can be

John Catto, Alpenglow Pictures

Dr. Ken Sims (right) and his associate, Dennis Jackson, sample gases and aerosols from inside the crater of Vulcan Masaya, Nicaragua. To get to this location, they descended over 200 meters (600 feet) into the volcano!

important clues in studying the history of Earth's climate. One of the ways in which scientists study climate changes is to analyze the chemicals trapped for millions of years in ice sheets in places such as Antarctica. They use a hollow drill to cut deep into the ice sheets, pulling out a cylindrical sample, or ice core. Heavy metals in the ice sheets are like fingerprints, Sims said. Scientists can determine whether lead in the ice core comes from human-made pollution such as factory smoke, or from natural sources such as volcanic eruptions. His findings may even provide important clues in solving the mystery about the extinction of the dinosaurs. "There is a debate over volcanoes or meteorites as the cause," Sims said.[2]

Inside the Volcano

To go down into a volcano and return safely requires a considerable amount of expertise, skill, and patience. The greatest dangers Sims and his colleagues face come from the volcano's crumbly, unstable walls. Falling rocks may hit them, or the climbing ropes may be cut by the sharp edges of cooled lava. However, they always have somebody on top of the volcano monitoring **seismic** activity. If the earth starts to tremble, they will get out of there fast!

WHAT KILLED THE DINOSAURS?

Sixty-five million years ago, something happened on Earth that killed all the dinosaurs—except those that became birds. And it was not just the dinosaurs; half of all the species on the planet also died.

For years, many scientists believed that the prime suspect in this ancient murder mystery was a huge meteor that struck the planet, leaving a giant crater in Mexico. The impact killed everything nearby. It also sent up a cloud of debris into the atmosphere that blocked the sun's rays. Earth became much cooler. Many plants, no longer able to get enough energy from the sun, died. The entire food chain was affected.

New research suggests that a series of enormous volcanic eruptions in India might have been the main culprit for the death of the dinosaurs. These eruptions, occurring between 63 million and 67 million years ago, created lava beds more than twice the size of Texas. Volcanologists estimate that the main phase of the eruption released ten times more climate-changing gases than the meteor impact in Mexico. Paleontologists digging in the lava beds found evidence that a mass extinction of microscopic shell-forming creatures occurred just after the main phase of the eruptions—300,000 years after the meteor impact.[3]

It could be that a volcano did the dinosaurs in. Or maybe they were knocked out by the double whammy of the meteor impact and the volcano eruption.

Sims and the other scientists prepare for their descent into the volcano by setting up the ropes that will take them into and out of the crater. That can sometimes take most of the day. "Once your ropes are fixed, you can go up and down pretty regularly," Sims said. Carefully, they lower themselves and their instruments onto the floor of the crater. The descent can take up to two hours. Because the gases in the crater are toxic, they wear gas masks.

Once on the floor of the crater, they set up their scientific gear. Pumps suck the gas right out of the smoking vents, and instruments measure the composition of the gases. As they wait for the machines to collect and analyze the gas, the scientists might explore the crater, which is littered with sharp black and brown rocks, or collect the fine, thin pieces of lava called **Pele's hairs**. Often they put up an umbrella or look for shade, then read or do a crossword puzzle.

As the air turns cooler near the end of the day, the gas starts to condense. If Sims is not wearing a full-face gas mask, the vapor can begin to burn his eyes and skin. "It just gets miserable, and I don't have any desire to sleep down there," he said. So, as carefully as they descended, they climb back up to the top of the crater. Sometimes they camp in tents on the rim of the crater, only to get up the next morning and do it all again.

They are always mindful of the dangers. "We always hang extra ropes," Sims said, "in case two of you need to go up very quickly, or as a safety line for just one of us." Sims remembers sitting on the edge of a rim about 60 meters (200 feet) above a lava conduit in a volcano in Nicaragua. Two days later, the entire rim collapsed. "It's a changing, growing system," he said. "You're very careful about making the decision to go into a volcano."

Dangerous Volcanoes in the Congo

Sims traveled to the Democratic Republic of the Congo to study gas emissions from two of the most active volcanoes in Africa, Nyiragongo and Nyamuragira. These two volcanoes are responsible for nearly 40 percent of Africa's historical eruptions. Years of violent conflict in this part of the Congo have made it difficult for scientists to study the volcanoes, but understanding them is critical to ensure the safety of the people who live nearby. Nyiragongo, towering over the bustling city of Goma, is particularly dangerous.

Unlike Mount St. Helens or Vesuvius, Nyiragongo does not erupt with a big explosion. It erupts with big lava flows, like Hawaiian volcanoes. But Nyiragongo's eruptions are more dangerous because its lava is unusually thin and runny. "They call it black water," Sims said, and it can flow down the side of the volcano at speeds of up to 65 kilometers (40 miles) per hour. It is impossible to outrun. Nyiragongo erupted in 2002, burying much of Goma. It killed over 100 people and left 120,000 homeless.[4]

There is a web of cracks, or fissures, in the ground, spreading out from Nyiragongo's main crater. Eruptions can occur anywhere along those fissures— and Goma is built right on top of a fracture zone. Sims and other scientists fear that the next time Nyiragongo erupts, it could do so directly under the city.

Nyiragongo has become much more active within the last 100 years, and the local effects have been dramatic. It produces a tremendous amount of gas. "Around fifty percent of the world's sulfur dioxide is coming out of this volcano right now," Sims said. "The gas causes acid rain to fall, and you can see all of these big trees that have died because the acid rain kills everything."

Adding to the destruction, carbon dioxide and methane from the volcano seep into nearby Lake Kivu. For the time being, it sits harmlessly at the bottom. But if fast-moving lava from Nyiragongo were to flow into the lake, it could trigger the release of a cloud of gas that would suffocate thousands of people. In 1986, a much smaller lake in Cameroon, a country in western Africa, released a cloud of volcanic gas. More than 1,700 people died.[5]

The January 17, 2002, erupion of Nyiragongo covered over 18 percent of the surface of the city of Goma, in the Democratic Republic of the Congo. About three hundred thousand people were forced to evacuate.

A few miles away from Nyiragongo lies Nyamuragira. Like a competitive sibling, Nyamuragira has its own distinctive trait. While Nyiragongo emits huge amounts of gas, Nyamuragira produces more lava than any other volcano in Africa. It erupted in 2001, burning farmland, destroying trees, and polluting water supplies.

The greatest danger of studying Nyiragongo and especially Nyamuragira had nothing to do with the volcanoes themselves, but with the rebels waging war in that area. Armed bandits roam the region. It is a very dangerous part of the world. "No scientist had visited Nyamuragira for years," Sims said, "because it's been a rebel stronghold, and it's just been too risky to go there." With the rebels pushed back, at least for a time, in 2007, Sims and his team trekked to Nyamuragira. Heavily armed guards accompanied them.

"I went there to measure the gases from these volcanoes," Sims said, "and came back with a whole new perspective. We have two major volcanoes threatening the Democratic Republic of the Congo, where 4 million people have been killed in a civil war. There's a humanitarian crisis, and a major volcanic crisis would make it even worse."

Back in the Lab

While the fieldwork can certainly be an adventure, most of the real science takes place in the laboratory, Sims said. "None of that work bears fruit if you're not willing to sit down with a computer, or just a piece of paper, and think hard about what you're doing. You sit down with the data, you make computer models, you do the math. I've never met a great scientist who couldn't sit down and focus at a desk."

As a boy, Sims always figured his career would have something to do with the natural world. After being a professional climbing guide, he decided to go back to school to study geology. He watched a documentary called *Nature: The Volcano Watchers*, by the French scientists and moviemakers Maurice and Katia Krafft. "Their film was just phenomenal," Sims said. Studying volcanoes was the perfect career for a young man with a love of mountain climbing and a fascination with the way the earth works.

Would-be volcanologists should follow their hearts and "go for it," he said. "There is always a place for people who are good and willing to work hard."

CHAPTER 7

Fire in the Ocean

The deep seafloor, miles below the surface of the ocean, is one of the last great frontiers on Earth. It has rugged mountain ranges, trenches deep enough to swallow the highest peaks on land, and volcanoes both active and extinct. Robert Embley, a marine geologist with the United States National Oceanographic and Atmospheric Administration (NOAA), has spent his career developing new ways of exploring the bottom of the ocean. "There is so much that is unknown about the ocean floor," Embley said. "We're still finding stuff that blows us away."[1] Chief among those things: a close-up view of a furiously erupting underwater, or submarine, volcano.

Exploring New Frontiers

Like many scientists of his generation, when Robert Embley was a child, he wanted to be an astronaut. "The whole idea of exploration really appealed to me," he said. Somewhere along the way, he decided to become an **oceanographer** instead. It was a very good choice for a would-be explorer. In many ways the deep ocean was less understood than space, and it remains so today.

Embley studied geology in college, and then earned a Ph.D. in marine geology. As part of his education, he went on a lot of research cruises. It was only after he moved to NOAA's Pacific Marine Environmental Laboratory in Oregon that he began studying deep-sea volcanoes. NOAA had just developed a new **sonar** system that could map wide areas of the ocean floor at a time. This was an improvement on the older sonar technology that allowed scientists to map just one point at a time.

Dr. Robert Embley (left) and a colleague use a CTD (conductivity, temperature, depth) instrument to map hydrothermal plumes. The gray bottles sample the water column for chemistry.

Sixty to seventy percent of the earth's volcanic activity is on the ocean floor. Then, as now, very little was known about this hidden world. "We knew that there had to be a lot of eruptions going on, probably one a month, but we didn't know where they were, because we couldn't hear them," Embley said.

Embley and his colleagues focused their studies on a **mid-ocean ridge** 400 kilometers (250 miles) off the coast of Oregon and Washington. The Juan de Fuca Ridge, as it is known, is part of an underwater volcanic mountain range. The range is more than 64,000 kilometers (40,000 miles) long and circles most of the globe, from the Arctic through the Atlantic, Indian, and Pacific oceans.

An Underwater Volcano Observatory

The Juan de Fuca Ridge is between two tectonic plates that are slowly moving apart in a stop-and-go kind of way. When they move, there are thousands of small

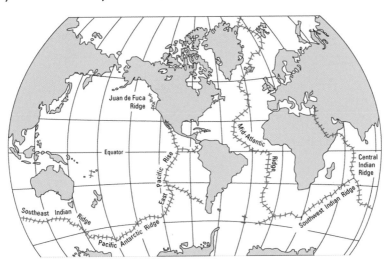

The mid-ocean ridge wraps around the globe like the seam on a baseball.

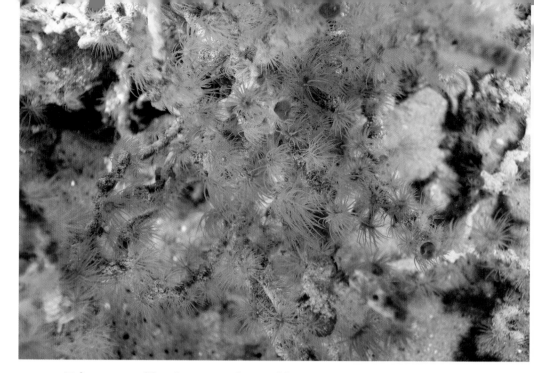

Tubeworms, like the ones pictured here at a seafloor hot spring on Daikoku volcano, only live at hydrothermal vents.

earthquakes and volcanic eruptions. The lava fills in the widening gap with new crust. Embley and other NOAA scientists set up an underwater volcano observatory called NeMO (New Millennium Observatory). NeMO is near the Axial Seamount, a very active volcano. Once a year, a team of scientists, engineers, teachers, and crew embark on a research cruise to NeMO. Using a remote-controlled submarine and many other instruments, they are studying the ways in which deep-sea volcanic activity affects the surrounding area.

The volcano and its hot springs are warm spots on the cold, barren ocean floor. The area provides a thriving habitat for a host of creatures. There are microbes that live off the iron sulfide and hydrogen sulfide spewing out of the vents. They are among the most ancient forms of life. Some microbes even live under the seafloor.

These microbes, in turn, form the base of the food chain for larger creatures: exotic tubeworms that wave about in the ocean currents, clams, shrimp, mussels, anemones, and fish. These creatures are specially adapted to live in or near underwater volcanoes. Biologists want to learn how the animal population changes when there is an eruption, and what happens between eruptions. Embley and other geologists are researching how the seafloor moves as the crust stretches apart. By studying the area over many years, the NeMO team hopes to find the answers to these questions.

In 1998, the first year of the NeMO project, the scientists detected thousands of small earthquakes, and soon a lava flow emerged from a crack in the volcano. A seafloor-monitoring instrument called a rumbleometer became trapped in the lava flow. Amazingly, it survived. When scientists were able to free it from the lava, they retrieved a gold mine of data from the instrument. This was the first time

Workers on the research ship *Ronald H. Brown* lower a rumbleometer into the ocean to monitor volcanic activity on the sea floor.

anybody had caught a submarine volcano in the act of erupting.[2]

One of the really exciting things about these research cruises, Embley said, is that there are so many different kinds of scientists coming together to study the site. At the end of the three-week-long expedition, Embley, the chief scientist on the project that year, wrote in his cruise log, "On the last day of the voyage, we all gathered together to discuss the results. A feeling that everyone had was that the scientific success of the expedition was primarily because of interaction between the geologists, chemists, and biologists, made possible because of the ability of the [remotely operated vehicle] to bring us all to the seafloor at the same time."[3]

The Submarine Ring of Fire Expedition

Embley and other NOAA scientists have also begun research cruises to the Mariana Arc, a string of active volcanoes all the way on the other side of the Pacific Ocean. The Mariana Arc is part of a larger group of active volcanoes called the **Ring of Fire**, which also includes the Juan de Fuca Ridge.

The Ring of Fire partially encircles the Pacific Ocean Basin, from New Zealand, north to New Guinea, through Indonesia, the Philippines, Japan, and Russia. It continues across the Aleutian Islands, and south to the mountains along the western coasts of North and South America.

The volcanoes in the Mariana Arc are very different from those in the Juan de Fuca Ridge. These volcanoes are the result of tectonic plate collision. As one plate gets pushed beneath another, a trench forms. The magma below is released as the first plate sinks. It rises and may erupt violently to form volcanoes. Over time, some of these volcanoes grow and grow until they become islands. Some of Earth's most active—and dangerous—volcanoes are in the Mariana Arc.

While the frequent and sometimes very dangerous

KEEPING TABS ON KICK-'EM-JENNY

No one is quite sure how the underwater volcano Kick-'em-Jenny got its name, but it probably has something to do with the rough waters around the area. Kick-'em-Jenny is in the Caribbean Sea, just off the coast of the island of Grenada. At about 250 meters (820 feet) from the surface of the ocean, the volcano is an island in the making. It grows and grows with each eruption as volcanic deposits build up around its summit. The volcano has erupted at least twelve times since it was discovered in 1939, although the lava record tells scientists that it was active long before then.

Kick-'em-Jenny lies directly under a main island shipping route. Many people fish and sail in the area. If Kick-'em-

eruptions of the land-based volcanoes in the arc are closely monitored, until recently scientists knew very little about the arc's underwater volcanoes. They knew that the volcanoes in the arc were active—they had detected their rumblings with new underwater listening devices. Other than that, nothing much was known.

Embley and a team of scientists on the Submarine Ring of Fire Expedition set out to explore the Mariana Arc in 2003. On board the research vessel, the scientists used the latest seafloor mapping tools

Jenny erupts, it could throw hot rocks up through the water and high into the air. This would pose a great danger to nearby ships and boats.

Even when quiet, Kick-'em-Jenny can be dangerous. Sometimes underwater volcanoes release a lot of gas into the water. This makes the water above the vent less dense. If a boat happens to be in the area when this happens, it could sink.

In 2007, a team of scientists installed a new underwater earthquake monitoring system on top of Kick-'em-Jenny. The device collects data about the volcano's rumblings. It sends the information through a flexible, stretchy cable to instruments on a buoy on the surface of the sea. These instruments use power from the sun to transmit the data to a station on nearby Grenada.[4]

In the future, scientists hope, boats near Grenada will be warned in time to avoid Kick-'em-Jenny's kick.

and sensors to find more than fifty volcanoes. They could detect plumes of heat, gas, and metals. "We thought there must really be something going on here!" Embley said.

When the team returned to the area the next year, they had something new in their scientific toolbox. It was a remotely operated vehicle called ROPOS (Remotely Operated Platform for Ocean Science). ROPOS was attached to the ship by a cable, and controlled by a pilot on the ship. The vehicle had two robotic arms for taking samples of rocks or living creatures, a vacuum machine that could suck up mud and other things on the ocean floor, and bottles for collecting water samples and superhot vent fluids. Its two cameras could transmit live video back to scientists on the ship.

Embley and the other scientists returned to the spot where they had detected some of the greatest hydrothermal activity. They tracked a giant smoky plume of water and gas to a crater in the NW Rota-1 volcano. This was one of the hottest spots they had ever found on any submarine volcano! They named it Brimstone Pit. The next day, they sent ROPOS down to investigate. The scientists watched in amazement as Brimstone Pit spewed gas from a magma source lying directly below, and then pelted ROPOS, perched on its rim, with yellow balls of sulfur and chunks of black rock.[5]

It was not until 2006 that Embley and the Ring of Fire team could return to NW Rota-1 and Brimstone Pit. Excitement ran high: What would they find this year? They sent down a new remotely operated vehicle, the *Jason II*, down to check it out. The volcano did not disappoint them. It was more active than ever!

"We saw huge steam explosions and glowing red lava jetting out of the vent," Embley said. While the violence of the eruption would have been more than enough to send scientists on land running for safety, the water pressure at Brimstone Pit dampened the explosion. This allowed the *Jason II* to get close enough to take samples from the erupting crater. "We couldn't have asked for a more ideal case," Embley said. There is a good chance, he added, that this is a long-term eruption that they can study for several years to come.

The fireworks display at Brimstone Pit was not the only surprise the scientists found on the 2006 expedition. They discovered a large pool of liquid sulfur, a window into the subsurface plumbing of the volcano. They saw a volcano, NW Eifuku, that vented carbon dioxide not in the familiar gas form, but as drops of liquid. Embley explained that the carbon dioxide was in liquid form in this spot because of the very high water pressure and low temperature. They found large beds of mussels nearby living off the carbon dioxide and other vent chemicals.

Carbon dioxide reacts with water to form an acid. This makes the area surrounding the NW Eifuku volcano more acidic. It also makes NW Eifuku a good laboratory to study the ways in which climate change might affect other ocean habitats. As rising levels of

These chimneys at the Champagne vent site in the NW Eifuku volcano are venting fluids at 103°C (217°F).

carbon dioxide in the atmosphere increase the ocean's acidity, some marine animals are having a hard time making shells, because the acid dissolves them. Coral reefs are in danger. Yet NW Eifuku's mussels thrive, despite the high acidity. How do they do it? Scientists are not sure, but as Embley said, "It's important to find this stuff sooner rather than later. It's going to teach us a lot about what's going on."

A Research Cruise Is Not a Vacation Cruise . . .

Embley said that their research cruises are typically three to five weeks long. The expeditions are very expensive, so every minute is precious. It is an around-the-clock operation, with most people working twelve- to eighteen-hour days. There may be twenty or twenty-five people in the scientific party—biologists, microbiologists, chemists, and geologists—and another ten people who operate the remotely operated vehicles or other technical equipment. As chief scientist on many of the cruises, Embley coordinates all the dives and the demands of the many different projects. "When you're exploring, you can't really plan very far ahead," he said. "It's very intense, and sometimes it can be pretty overwhelming."

Embley's advice to an aspiring young oceanographer is to follow your dream. "I once had a teacher who told me, 'You'll never make a living doing this.' Rather a strange comment coming from a teacher! I'm not saying you should ignore everything your teacher says, but if you feel it's right and you want to do it, don't let anybody knock you down."

CHAPTER 8

Yellowstone: The Sleeping Giant

Millions of people visit Yellowstone National Park each year. They come for a glimpse of buffalo, elk, bears, and maybe even wolves. They marvel at the spectacular Old Faithful geyser, bubbling mud pots, and smelly hot springs made colorful by the microbes living within. What many of those visitors do not realize is that they are inside the caldera of one of the world's largest volcanoes.

"Not all volcanoes look the same," said Lisa Morgan, a geologist with the U.S. Geological Survey in Colorado. "The deal with Yellowstone is that it's such a big volcano that you don't really see it unless you know what you're looking for."[1]

Scientists do not believe Yellowstone will erupt any time soon, but it is active. Morgan is one of the scientists studying and monitoring the giant volcano for signs of increased restlessness. She explained that the North American tectonic plate is slowly moving over a hot spot in the earth's mantle, and "burning a big hole in the crust, so to speak."

The park's many geothermal features—geysers, mud pots, and hot springs among them—are fueled by heat from a huge magma chamber just a few miles below the surface. The Yellowstone region has produced three exceedingly large volcanic eruptions in the past 2.1 million years. The latest eruption, which occurred 640,000 years ago, ejected 8,000 times the amount of ash and lava of Mount St. Helens. The loss of such large volumes of magma caused the surrounding ground to collapse. This created a broad crater, or caldera. The most recent eruption made a

Lisa Morgan does fieldwork on the margins of the eastern Snake River Plain, where old Yellowstone-like calderas are buried.

caldera about 80 kilometers (50 miles) long and 56 kilometers (35 miles) wide.[2] The entire Snake River Plain, stretching about 640 kilometers (400 miles) west of Yellowstone all the way to the Idaho-Oregon border, is a broad, flat valley. It is made of old calderas that were formed as the continent moved over the hot spot.

Thar She Blows?

Scientists say that the Yellowstone caldera will almost certainly erupt again someday. It is possible that a future eruption will reach the magnitude of those three enormous eruptions. If it does, it would bury a large part of the United States in thick ash deposits, and it would drastically affect global climate. There is no reason to cancel your Yellowstone vacation, though. Morgan said the caldera shows no signs that it is headed for a gigantic eruption.

Far more likely are slow-moving lava flows or explosions of hot groundwater (hydrothermal explosions). The magma chamber beneath Yellowstone heats the surrounding rocks. As melted snow and rainwater seep deep into the ground, this water—called groundwater—heats up. Pockets of water can suddenly come to a boil and explode as the water turns to steam. These explosions are what make Old Faithful and other geysers in the park erupt.

Occasionally, the heated groundwater boils where the steam has no opening from which to escape. The steam builds and builds until the pressure becomes so great that it blows a big hole in the ground above, hurling boiling water, steam, and rock thousands of feet into the air. One such explosion happened about 13,800 years ago, Morgan said, near the northeastern edge of Yellowstone Lake. This explosion created a crater 2.4 kilometers (1.5 miles) in diameter.

"It looks like the Cookie Monster took a big bite out of the lake," she said.

When the Porkchop Geyser in Norris Basin became plugged up in 1989, a small hydrothermal explosion rained rocks on tourists some 180 meters (200 yards) away. Morgan and her colleagues are trying to better understand the possible warning signs of such an event. "This is probably one of the most challenging things right now. There has not been a lot of work on these large hydrothermal explosions;

After becoming blocked in 1989, Porkchop Geyser exploded and spewed rocks up to 200 yards away.

Porkchop Geyser after its explosion

we've never experienced one in front of us. We're really just learning about them."

From Cutthroat Trout to a Geological Discovery

The National Park Service had a problem. The cutthroat trout, once the most common and widely distributed native trout in Yellowstone Lake, was in serious trouble. Someone—no one knows who—had illegally put some lake trout into Yellowstone Lake. "The lake trout is a very aggressive fish," says Morgan. "It is estimated that one lake trout eats about fifty cutthroat trout each year, and that is having a devastating effect on the population."

Like salmon, the cutthroat trout swims upstream into one of the many rivers that flow into the lake to spawn, or lay its eggs. During this time, it is a very important food source for grizzly bears, otters, osprey, and bald eagles. In contrast, the lake trout stays in the lake its entire life. "There's nothing to replace the cutthroat trout as a key food source for these species," Morgan says.

Fish biologists needed a more accurate map to help them figure out where the lake trout were spawning. The National Park Service asked Morgan and her colleagues to create a map of the bottom of Yellowstone Lake. The lake had been surveyed in 1871, and again in the 1980s. Even though both surveys had used the most up-to-date technology of the times, the maps were not very precise.

In 1999 the scientists began using a variety of high-tech approaches to map the lake floor, including a global positioning device, sonar, and a remotely operated underwater vehicle. It took them four summers to complete the map. While the 1871 survey collected 300 data points, Morgan and her team ended up with over 240 million data points.

What they found was as interesting for the geologists as it was for the fish biologists. The biggest surprise: a bulge the size of seven football fields rising 100 feet above the lake floor. They found old lava flows from the latest caldera-forming eruption and craters formed by past hydrothermal explosions. They found hundreds of hot springs, vents, and spire-shaped structures that spewed out fluids rich in hydrogen sulfide. These areas are havens for sulfur-eating bacteria and the creatures that feed on them. In a news report, one scientist said of the lake bottom's features: "It would be the most spectacular part of the park, if you could see it."[3]

Morgan calls the bulge the inflated plain, and it appears to be the result of steam or carbon dioxide gas building up under the lakebed, sealed in by sediments and water pressure. If the dome blows its top in a giant hydrothermal explosion—and Morgan thinks it might—it would create a giant wave of water and steam, throwing rocks the size of trucks into the air, and carving another gigantic crater into the floor of Yellowstone Lake. You would not want to be there when it happened.

Still, Morgan sees no signs that it is ready to blow any time soon. They remapped the dome in 2002, three years after they originally discovered it. They wanted to see if the structure was growing, shrinking, or changing shape. Because they were not able to detect any differences, they concluded that the dome—for the time being, anyway—is fairly stable. They also sent their remotely operated vehicle down to collect fluids and gases to check for changes in activity; they found nothing new. But the scientists continue to keep a close eye on the lake dome and other potential sites of hydrothermal explosions. Morgan said they are still developing new ways to monitor the park's hydrothermal features. "We do know that these explosions are more likely to occur sometime in the fall, when the systems tend to heat up," she said.

Will Yellowstone Erupt Again?

Morgan emphasized that a hydrothermal explosion is not necessarily a sign of a coming volcanic eruption. "We have no interaction of water and magma in the park," she said in a talk she gave at Yellowstone.[4]

A better sign of a future large, explosive eruption would be a dramatic shift in the ground level at Yellowstone. Scientists monitoring the area know that the movements of gas, magma, or water under Earth's crust cause the caldera to rise and fall, like the chest of a sleeping giant (see "Monitoring the Volcano's

Breath" on page 96). This is normal. A big change in the caldera's "breathing" patterns is one warning sign that a large amount of new magma is rising into the chamber.

Scientists would also look for increased swarms of earthquakes. Normally, 1,000 to 3,000 small earthquakes to shake Yellowstone each year. More frequent, and shallower, earthquakes would alert scientists to the presence of rising magma under the crust.

Last of all, the scientists would notice a change in the gases coming from the park's many **fumaroles** (vents from which volcanic gases escape into the atmosphere) and hot springs. Morgan said that all of these warning signs would build up decades, if not hundreds of years, before a catastrophic eruption.

Art Rocks!

Mapping the floor of Yellowstone Lake was "probably one of the most fun projects I have ever been involved in," Morgan said. "It was like having a new discovery every day." But being a rock detective—which is how Morgan thinks of herself—is nearly always exciting. "It's a great job," she said. "I look at the rocks and the associated structures and try to figure out what they

MONITORING THE VOLCANO'S BREATH

Q: *How do you monitor a sleeping giant?*
A: *Very carefully!*

Although monitoring the rise and fall of Yellowstone does require careful work, it has nothing to do with disturbing the caldera. It is just the nature of volcanology.

Scientists at the United States Geological Survey and the University of Utah found that from 2004 through 2006, the floor of the caldera rose almost 7 centimeters (3 inches) each year.[5] This does not seem like a lot, but it is more than three times greater than ever observed since such measurements began in 1923.

The scientists used two techniques to make their measurements. They first used images from the European Space Agency's satellite *Envisat*. Each time the satellite

are and how they got here, which is a lot of fun. It's very important to learn how to observe."

Morgan, who is also an artist, knows a lot about the importance of looking at things carefully. She grew up camping and backpacking with her father and siblings in Rocky Mountain National Park in Colorado. "I can remember climbing my very first volcano there," she said. "It had all of these false summits, and cinder. I thought it was really cool."

passed over Yellowstone, an instrument on board aimed pulses of radar energy at the floor of the caldera. The signal that bounced back to the satellite gave a very detailed picture of the whole caldera. By comparing the images from one year to the next, scientists could see how the caldera was changing.

To get a more detailed picture of the moving caldera, the scientists also used twelve Global Positioning System (GPS) ground stations placed around the caldera. Each GPS station "listens to" a network of satellites orbiting Earth. The satellites send information back to the GPS stations, telling them exactly where they are. (These are more precise versions of the GPS systems used in cars.)

One of the scientists on the study is Robert B. Smith, a professor of geophysics at the University of Utah. "Our best evidence is that the crustal magma chamber is filling with molten rock," he says. But that does not mean there will be an eruption soon. "A lot of calderas worldwide go up and down over decades without erupting."[6]

But she never planned to become a geologist; instead, she wanted to be an artist. As an art major in college, she thought that learning more about the science behind color and light would help her painting, so she took a geology class about minerals and crystals. "I was pretty much hooked on geology," she said. After college, she earned a Ph.D. in geology and geophysics from the University of Hawaii.

In many ways, Morgan still thinks like an artist.

And as far as she is concerned, this is perfectly natural. Both artists and scientists learn to look at the world in great detail. They find things that less careful observers might not see. "People are sometimes surprised to hear this science-art connection, but it makes total sense to me," she said. "I don't think you can do science and not be a creative person."

CHAPTER 9

A Volcano SWAT Team That Saves Lives

On April 2, 1991, Mount Pinatubo in the Philippines began to stir with a swarm of earthquakes and steam explosions. The volcano had been dormant for 500 years, and many people believed it to be harmless. Some did not even recognize it as a volcano.

Over the years it had become worn down. It no longer resembled the steep-sided cone volcanoes nearby. Thirty thousand people lived in small villages on the flanks of Mount Pinatubo. Another 500,000 lived in cities and villages on the plains surrounding it. They would surely be in grave danger if Pinatubo erupted.

The most likely explanation for the seismic stirrings in 1991 was that magma was rising within the volcano. They could be signals of a potentially disastrous eruption. But when and how big would it be?

Native homes near Mount Pinatubo were destroyed during its eruption in June, 1991.

Ray Punongbayan, director of the Philippine Institute of Volcanology and Seismology, contacted his friend Chris Newhall, a scientist at the United States Geological Survey (USGS). Punongbayan had an experienced team of scientists, but he had a feeling that they would need reinforcements. Could Newhall send a team to help monitor the volcano's activity?[1]

The answer was yes. Newhall and a handful of other USGS volcanologists flew to the Philippines immediately. They formed a volcano emergency team that eventually came to be called the Volcano Disaster Assistance Program (VDAP) team. Together with the Filipino scientists, the VDAP team looked at signs left from ancient eruptions. They determined that an eruption would threaten Clark United States Air Force Base, as well as tens of thousands of people living near the volcano. They installed instruments to detect earthquakes and signs of the ground rising—clues of restless magma underneath.

By early June of that year, the scientists could tell that an eruption could begin at any time. Philippine officials evacuated about a million people from around the volcano. On June 12, Pinatubo blew its top. The eruptions lasted for several days, with a huge blast on June 15 that sent a column of ash

This photo of the June 12, 1991 eruption of Mount Pinatubo was taken from the east side of Clark Air Base.

40 kilometers (25 miles) into the air. The drifting ash cloud damaged more than twenty passenger jets, even though most of them were flying more than 960 kilometers (600 miles) from the volcano. Pyroclastic flows, ash, and pumice soon engulfed the area. That same day, a typhoon brought heavy rain. The water-soaked ash flowed down into the valleys in great lahars, wiping out farmland and entire villages. The mudflows

lasted for months, and they continue to be a problem whenever the monsoons come and drench the disturbed landscape.

This was the largest eruption in eighty years. Material from the eruption circled the globe within a week. It caused global cooling for up to five years. The surrounding villages, home to about seventy thousand people, were completely destroyed. But the advance warning saved the lives of hundreds of thousands of people. It gave the United States Air Force a chance to move millions of dollars' worth of aircraft and equipment to safety.

The SWAT Team

John Pallister, the chief of the Volcano Disaster Assistance Program, called it "arguably the best, most successful volcano response that anybody knows of."[2] VDAP, based at the Cascades Volcano Observatory in Vancouver, Washington, is a kind of volcano SWAT team. The team members stand by, ready to lend a hand—sometimes on very short notice—to help predict and monitor volcanic eruptions worldwide. "Our first responsibility is to help save lives," Pallister said. "And the second is to improve our ability to do the first by understanding how volcanoes work."

Dr. John Pallister collects rock samples from Mount St. Helens.

The idea for the Volcano Disaster Assistance Program originally came about after a disastrous eruption of Nevado del Ruiz in Colombia in 1985.[3] An eruption at the summit of this steep-sided volcano sent avalanches of hot volcanic debris and clouds of ash and gas across the snow pack. The snow and ice melted and flooded down the sides of the mountain. The water picked up loose rocks and dirt as it went, traveling at speeds of up to 50 kilometers (30 miles) per hour. Most people in the town of Armero were asleep when the hot lahar reached them, two and one-half hours after the volcano erupted. In a few minutes, most of the town was swept away or buried in a layer of mud and boulders. More than twenty-three thousand people lost their lives.

That was before Pallister became involved with the program, but he said that it was a real eye-opener for both geologists and emergency managers. "With good monitoring and an understanding of the hazards posed by these snow-clad volcanoes, people could have been evacuated to high ground, and many lives would have been saved," he said.

Pallister was not part of the original VDAP team that responded to the Pinatubo eruption. Instead, he was part of a team that came to the volcano afterward to carry out some detective work, trying to figure out why it erupted. In the end, he said, the volcanologists learned a lot about the science behind these types of volcanic eruptions.

Since that time, VDAP has responded to many volcano crises around the world. "In the early years of the program, there were lots of emergency responses where we sent teams of scientists to help our counterparts set up monitoring stations and observatories," he said. "Today, many more countries have good volcano observatories, and they have very capable scientists. They may only need special instruments or additional people to help in a crisis. In

PREDICTING VOLCANIC ERUPTIONS

Seismometers can detect and record vibrations in the earth. A series of small, intense earthquakes—up to several hundred per hour—can often signal the beginnings of a volcanic eruption.

When magma begins to rise into the region just beneath a volcano, it changes the shape of the volcano. The changes usually cannot be seen with the naked eye, but volcanologists have very sensitive instruments that can help them measure these changes. Tilt meters have pendulums that measure the differences in the slope of a volcano. There are often cracks in the earth around volcanoes; these tend to widen as the magma rises. Displacement meters measure the changes in these cracks. Volcano craters also become larger before an eruption, sometimes just by millimeters. Scientists use electronic distance meters to measure the diameter of a volcano's crater. And by using Global Positioning System stations set up on the flanks of volcanoes, scientists can use satellites orbiting Earth to detect movement around the volcano.

When magma rises into the chambers just below the volcano, it really heats things up. Nearby fumaroles and hot springs get warmer. There are changes in the gases coming out of the volcanoes. By putting put all these clues together, volcanologists can forecast volcanic eruptions.

an ideal world, our counterparts in other countries would be fully equipped and we wouldn't need to go. We're trying to work ourselves out of business."

In a real crunch, a VDAP team can be ready to go in a couple of days. Some take as long as a week to get organized. "We have to get the appropriate political clearances to travel, organize the equipment we'll take, buy plane tickets," Pallister said. "It's like a fire drill that lasts a few days. And fortunately, we usually have an advance warning of a few weeks or even months."

Unrest at Mount Merapi

Pallister's most memorable VDAP response came in 2006. He and a team of other scientists were on their way to help design a new volcano observatory on an island in Indonesia when they got a call. They were needed on Java, another Indonesian island. Mount Merapi was showing new signs of unrest. With 100,000 people living on the flanks of the volcano, and another million people in the nearby city of Yogyakarta, Mount Merapi is one of the most dangerous volcanoes in Indonesia.

Scientists at the Merapi Volcano Observatory had detected a rapidly growing bulge in the volcano, a sign that magma was rising to dangerously shallow levels. The bulge—and Merapi's history of deadly eruptions—had the scientists worried. Would it erupt in a gigantic explosion, as Mount St. Helens had done in 1980? "It was a difficult time," Pallister said, "trying to help deal with a tremendous threat to a whole lot of people in the area."

The VDAP team and the Indonesian scientists watched as the lava finally broke through the surface, and the volcano stopped bulging. "That meant that the pressure [in the volcano] was being relieved, and we all breathed a sigh of great relief," Pallister said. "We knew that we were looking at a lava emission, but not a collapse that could kill thousands of people." They issued evacuation warnings for the areas they knew would be affected by the lava flows. In the end, only two people who had refused to leave the area were killed.

"There is kind of a lesson for Americans in general," Pallister said. "Most of our volcanoes are on federal lands, or in parks or monuments, or in the Aleutian Islands where not many people live. It's a very different world to be working in a country like Indonesia that has something like one hundred sixty active volcanoes, and an average of ten to twelve eruptions a year. And at least half, if not most, of those eruptions threaten large numbers of people."

One of the most difficult parts of the job, Pallister continued, is making the right call at the right time. "One of the worst things we can do is to have people evacuate too soon. They get tired of waiting for the volcano to erupt and then move back at the wrong time. It's the 'boy who cried wolf' scenario. Volcanoes are kind of like tornadoes or hurricanes: You can see them coming, and you can give warnings. But we cannot predict how big the eruption will be. Merapi has had very large eruptions in the past, and so we knew it had the potential to do that again. But in the end, it was a very modest eruption. That's just what we have to live with."

Watching Mount St. Helens

When he is not responding to volcano crises in other parts of the world, Pallister and his colleagues at the Cascades Volcano Observatory continue to keep a close eye on Mount St. Helens. After its huge explosion in 1980, the volcano began to erupt again in 2004. But Pallister said it has been a remarkably non-explosive eruption so far. "It's producing a new lava dome," he said. The dome is replacing the part of the volcano that was blown away in the last eruption, although at this rate it will be many decades before it reaches its old height. For scientists like Pallister, it is an ideal laboratory for learning more about what triggers explosive eruptions. Mount St. Helens is not in any danger of having a dangerous eruption in the short term. But, Pallister said, it is "fully capable of producing another 1980-type eruption in the next few decades."

Rocks That Move

"I always wanted to figure out how things worked on the earth," Pallister said. "I started off studying geology in Georgia when I was in college. The more I learned about rocks, the more I became fascinated by the ones that moved—glaciers and volcanoes."

Throughout college and graduate school, he found himself studying all kinds of different volcanoes. He studied an ancient, extinct caldera in the San Juan Mountains in Colorado and took part in a drilling project to study the ocean crust and mantle in the Mid-Atlantic Ridge. His research finally brought him to the Cascades Volcano Observatory in Washington.

Young people who are interested in studying volcanoes should have a strong background in science and mathematics, and should enjoy a hands-on approach to solving problems. "A lot of what we do requires setting up remote field monitors using solar panels, or building communications networks to monitor places that are remote to us. Of course, you need to have a healthy curiosity about the way the earth works."

VDAP scientists must also understand how to communicate with people of many different cultures. "We don't stand in the foreground; we stand in the background," Pallister said. "Our job is to support and build credibility and capability in our counterparts. I think that VDAP plays a very strong role in international diplomacy. We can help each other with the mutual goal of saving lives and property, and that's something that cuts across all cultures throughout the world. It makes us better citizens of the world, and helps us build lasting relationships. It's nice to be part of a program that really does build an international network of friendships."

CHAPTER 10

So YOU Want to Be a Volcanologist?

Volcanologists are geologists who specialize in studying volcanoes and volcanic eruptions. While studying actively erupting volcanoes can certainly be exciting, most volcanologists spend only a small fraction of their time doing so. Volcano scientists spend much of their time studying the products that remain from the eruptions of extinct or dormant volcanoes. They analyze field data or samples in the laboratory and use computers to model eruptions. They read and write scientific papers. Because their research directly affects the lives of people living near volcanoes, many volcanologists work to educate and update local residents, community officials, journalists, and politicians about volcanic hazards.

Most volcanologists combine a love of the outdoors and desire to travel with an intense curiosity about the way the earth works. In high school, you will need a strong background in physics, chemistry, mathematics, and computer science. Knowledge of a second language is a good idea, since volcanologists often do a lot of traveling abroad. Strong communication and writing skills are important tools for any scientist.

There are no colleges or universities that offer a four-year bachelor's degree specifically in volcanology. Many—but not all—volcano scientists begin their careers with a degree in geology, geochemistry, or geophysics. Most volcano scientists also earn at least a master's degree (one to three years of study) or a Ph.D. (three to six additional years), doing more specialized coursework and research. Many scientists also do something called a postdoctoral fellowship, or "postdoc," after they receive their Ph.D.

For volcanologists, this is basically a two- to three-year paid research job at a university, volcano observatory, or geological survey company. Many postdocs with university positions also teach.

Scientists who study volcanoes focus on a variety of areas. Physical volcanologists study the actual workings and deposits of volcanic eruptions. Geophysicists might monitor seismic activity to help predict volcanic eruptions. Other volcanologists specialize in studying how the earth changes shape in relation to volcanic activity. Geochemists study the makeup of the earth and its products, including volcanic gases. There is always a need for technical support people, especially computer and electronics specialists.

Most people who become volcanologists do so because they are passionate about studying volcanoes, not to become rich. Volcanologists working at a United States university or government agency might earn $40,000 to $135,000 a year, depending on their level of education and experience.[1]

While volcano scientists are sometimes portrayed in the movies as daredevils, the truth is that most volcanologists take safety very seriously. They understand the power and potential destructiveness of volcanoes and do not take foolish chances.

Still, volcanoes can sometimes be unpredictable. A few scientists, like Dave Johnston, have died while studying volcanoes and working to make life safer for those living near them.

Visiting Volcanoes

If you think you might be interested in becoming a volcanologist, consider visiting a volcano. Many active volcanoes are generally safe for visitors. If they are not, scientists will make sure that tourists do not

Tourists walk on top of lava flowing from Kilauea Volcano in Hawaii Volcanoes National Park.

enter dangerous areas. Tourists flock to famous volcanoes around the world, from Vesuvius in Italy to Mount Fuji in Japan. There are many spectacular volcanoes in United States national parks, too.

The Hawaii Volcanoes National Park is very popular with tourists, who often see amazing and beautiful eruptions at very close range. The world's largest dome volcano is in Lassen Volcanic National Park in California. There, steaming fumaroles on the summit and many interesting geothermal areas are on display. Yellowstone National Park is the world's first national park. It is the most famous and most widely visited volcanic area in the United States. Despite the crowds, it is well worth a trip. Visitors may be drenched with spray from the Old Faithful geyser, smell sulfur bubbling from the mud pots, and see the gemlike green-and-blue hot springs, all fueled by the volcano below.

Chapter Notes

Chapter 1. Windows Into the Earth

1. Richard V. Fisher, Grant Heiken, and Jeffrey B. Hulen, *Volcanoes: Crucibles of Change* (Princeton, N.J.: Princeton University Press, 1997), p. 26.
2. "Mount St. Helens—From the 1980 Eruption to 2000," *U.S. Geological Survey Fact Sheet 036-00; Online Version 1.0*, <http://pubs.usgs.gov/fs/2000/fs036-00/>
3. Fisher, Heiken, and Hulen, p. 182.
4. Fisher, Heiken, and Hulen, pp. 4–6.
5. Jelle Zeilinga de Boer and Donald Theodore Sanders, *Volcanoes in Human History: The Far-Reaching Effects of Major Eruptions* (Princeton, N.J.: Princeton University Press, 2002), pp. 138–155.
6. Fisher, Heiken, and Hulen, pp. 123–125.
7. Robert I. Tilling, *Volcanoes*, U.S. Geological Survey, 1997, p. 1. <http://pubs.usgs.gov/gip/volc/>.
8. Jacques-Marie Bardintzeff and Alexander R. McBirney, *Volcanology* (Boston: Jones & Bartlett Publishers, 2000), p. 248.
9. Ibid., p. 249.

Chapter 2. What Are Volcanoes and Why Do They Erupt?

1. Robert Decker and Barbara Decker, *Volcanoes* (New York: W.H. Freeman and Company, 2006), p. 154–173.
2. Jacob B. Lowenstern, et. al., "Steam Explosions, Earthquakes, and Volcanic Eruptions—What's in Yellowstone's Future?" *U.S. Geological Survey Fact Sheet 2005–3024* <http://pubs.usgs.gov/fs/2005/3024/>.

Chapter 3. Lessons from a Bronze Age Pompeii

1. Giuseppe Mastrolorenzo, et. al., "The Avellino 3780-yr-B.P. catastrophe as a worst-case scenario for a future eruption at

Vesuvius," *Proceedings of the National Academy of Sciences*, 103:4366–4370, March 13, 2006.

2. Giuseppe Mastrolorenzo, interview, June 15, 2007.
3. Lucia Pappalardo, interview, June 15, 2007.
4. Giuseppe Mastrolorenzo, interview, June 15, 2007.
5. Rosaly Lopes, *The Volcano Adventure Guide* (Cambridge, England: Cambridge University Press), 2005, p. 202.

Chapter 4. At Home with Pele

1. Jim Kauahikaua and G. Brad Lewis, *Volcano: Creation in Motion* (Honolulu, Hawaii: Mutual Publishing, 2004), p. 1.
2. Jim Kauahikaua, interview, September 21, 2007.
3. Rosaly Lopes, *The Volcano Adventure Guide* (Cambridge, England: Cambridge University Press, 2005), p. 69.
4. Christina Heliker, Donald A. Swanson, and Taeko Jane Takahashi, eds., Professional Paper 1676, "The Puʻu ʻOʻo-Kupaianaha Eruption of Kilauea Volcano, Hawaiʻi: The First 20 Years." U.S. Geological Survey: Reston, Va., 2003.
5. Kauahikaua and Lewis, p. 2.
6. "Explosive Eruptions at Kilauea Volcano, Hawaiʻi?", *U.S. Geological Survey Fact Sheet 132-98*, <http://pubs.usgs.gov/fs/fs132-98/>.
7. Jelle Zeilinga de Boer and Donald Theodore Sanders, *Volcanoes in Human History: The Far-Reaching Effects of Major Eruptions* (Princeton, N.J.: Princeton University Press, 2002), pp. 43–44.

Chapter 5. Volcanoes Are Out of This World!

1. Rosaly Lopes, "Io, a world of great volcanoes," *Volcanic Worlds: Exploring the Solar System's Volcanoes*, Rosaly M.C. Lopes and Tracy K.P. Gregg, eds. (Chichester, UK: Springer-Praxis Books in Geophysical Sciences, 2004), p. 127.
2. Ibid., p. 133.
3. Ibid., p. 139.

4. Itay Halevy, Maria T. Zuber, and Daniel P. Schrag, "A Sulfur Dioxide Climate Feedback on Early Mars," *Science*, 21 December 2007, pp. 1903–1907.
5. Rosaly Lopes, interview, July 24, 2007.
6. Rosaly Lopes, *The Volcano Adventure Guide* (Cambridge, England: Cambridge University Press, 2005), p. 217.

Chapter 6. Volcanoes Are a Gas!
1. Kenneth Sims, interview, August 8, 2007.
2. Chris Carroll, "Sniffing for Clues to Dinosaurs' Demise," *National Geographic*, October 2004, p. 4.
3. Gerta Keller, Thierry Adatte, and Sunil Bajpai, "Main Deccan Volcanism Phase Ends at K-T Mass Extinction: Evidence from the Krishna-Godavari Basin, SE India," *Abstract 136–13, 2007 Geological Society of America Annual Meeting*, Denver, October 28–31, 2007.
4. *NOVA*: "Volcano Under the City," WGBH Boston, 2006.
5. Ibid.

Chapter 7. Fire in the Ocean
1. Robert Embley, interview, September 17, 2007.
2. Christopher G. Fox, William W. Chadwick, and Robert W. Embley, "Direct observation of a submarine volcanic eruption from a sea-floor instrument caught in a lava flow," *Nature*, vol. 412, August 16, 2001, pp. 727–729.
3. Robert Embley, "NeMO Cruise 1998: September 20, 1998, Chief Scientist Final Report," http://www.pmel.noaa.gov/vents/nemo1998/science-news.html
4. "Real-time Seismic Monitoring Station Installed Atop Active Underwater Volcano," News release, Woods Hole Oceanographic Institution, May 10, 2007.
5. Robert W. Embley et. al., "Long-term Eruptive Activity at a Submarine Arc Volcano," *Nature*, vol. 441, May 25, 2006, pp. 494–497.

Chapter 8. Yellowstone: The Sleeping Giant

1. Lisa Morgan, interview, September 7, 2007.
2. Jacob B. Lowenstern, et. al., "Steam Explosions, Earthquakes, and Volcanic Eruptions—What's in Yellowstone's Future?" *U.S. Geological Survey Fact Sheet 2005–3024* <http://pubs.usgs.gov/fs/2005/3024/>.
3. Kevin Krajick, "Thermal Features Bubble in Yellowstone Lake," *Science*, Vol. 292, May 25, 2001, pp. 1479–1480.
4. Lisa Morgan, "The floor of Yellowstone Lake is anything but quiet: Volcanic and hydrothermal processes in a large lake above a magma chamber," February 10, 2004, <http://www.nps.gov/yell/naturescience/transcriptmorgan.htm>.
5. Wu-Lung Chang et. al., "Accelerated Uplift and Magmatic Intrusion of the Yellowstone Caldera, 2004 to 2006," *Science*, vol. 316, November 9, 2007, pp. 952–956.
6. Press release, University of Utah Public Relations, November 8, 2007, <http://www.eurekalert.org/pub_releases/2007-11/uou-yr103007.php>.

Chapter 9. A Volcano SWAT Team That Saves LIves

1. Dick Thompson, *Volcano Cowboys: The Rocky Evolution of a Dangerous Science* (New York: St. Martin's Press, 2002), p. 210.
2. John Pallister, interview, September 10, 2007.
3. John W. Ewert, et. al., "Mobile Response Team Saves Lives in Volcano Crises," *U.S. Geological Survey Fact Sheet 064-97*, <http://pubs.usgs.gov/fs/1997/fs064-97/>.

Chapter 10. So You Want to Be a Volcanologist?

1. Bureau of Labor Statistics, U.S. Department of Labor, *Occupational Outlook Handbook, 2008–2009 Edition*, Geoscientists, <http://www.bls.gov/oco/ococ288.htm> (accessed March 24, 2008).

Glossary

'a'a (AH ah)—A Hawaiian word for lava flows that have a rough, rubbly surface made of cooled areas of lava.

ash—Very fine volcanic rock, mineral, and glass fragments.

bomb (BAHM)—A large lava fragment ejected while it is still partly molten, or melted.

caldera (kal DER uh)—The Spanish word for cauldron; a large basin-shaped depression formed when huge volumes of magma are erupted, leading to the collapse of the rock above.

cinder cone (SIN dur kohn)—A steep, cone-shaped hill of volcanic fragments that accumulates around a vent.

crater (KRAY tur)—A bowl-shaped opening at the top of a volcano.

crust (KRUST)—The layer of rocks that form the continents and the areas of shallow seabed close to their shores.

cryovolcano (KRYE oh vawl KAY noh)—An icy volcano on other planets or moons that erupt very cold mixtures of water, ammonia, or methane.

excavation (EK skuh VAY shun)—The site of an archaeological dig.

fumarole (FYOO muh rohl)—A vent from which volcanic gases escape into the atmosphere.

hot spot—A fixed spot located above a hot plume of magma that is breaking through Earth's mantle.

isotope (EYE suh tohp)—One of the different forms of atoms of the same element. Isotopes have the same number of protons in their nuclei, but a different number of neutrons.

lahar (LAH hahr)—A rapidly flowing mixture of rock, debris, and water that started out on the slopes of a volcano. Also called a mudflow.

lapilli (luh PIHL eye, sing.: lapillus)—Small rock fragments ejected from a volcano during an explosive eruption.

lava (LAH vuh)—Molten rock that erupts from a volcanic vent. Geologists also use the word to describe the solid deposits of lava flows and fragments hurled into the air.

lava tube—A tunnel formed when the surface of a lava flow cools and becomes solid while the still-molten lava underneath flows through and drains away.

magma (MAG muh)—Molten or partially molten rock containing dissolved gases and crystals beneath the earth's surface.

magma chamber—An underground cavity that supplies magma to the volcano.

mantle (MAN tuhl)—The part of the earth below the crust and above the core.

mid-ocean ridge (MIHD oh shun RIHJ)—A mountain range with a central valley on an ocean floor at the boundary between two separating tectonic plates, and where magma from Earth's interior can move toward the surface, forming new crust.

ocean crust—The earth's crust where it lies under oceans.

oceanographer (OH shun AH gruh fur)—A scientist who studies the ocean's physical features and the living things in it.

pahoehoe (puh HOH eh hoh eh)—A Hawaiian word for lava that has a smooth, billowy, or ropy surface.

Pele's hairs (PEH lehz HAIRZ)—Thick strands of volcanic glass drawn out from molten lava. Small bits of round or tear-shaped particles, often found on one end of a strand of Pele's hair, are called **Pele's tears**.

plate tectonics (PLAYT tehk TAH nihks)—The theory that Earth's crust is broken into fragments, or plates, that move in relation to one another.

plume (PLOOM)—A turbulent flow of volcanic particles, gas, and air that rises into the atmosphere after an eruption.

pumice (PUM ihs)—A light volcanic rock that forms during explosive eruptions. It resembles a sponge because it contains a network of bubbles formed by trapped gas. It is so light that it can float on water.

pyroclastic flow (PYE roh KLAS tihk FLOH)—An avalanche of hot ash, pumice, rock fragments, and gas that rushes down the side of a volcano. It is one of the greatest hazards of volcanic eruptions.

pyroclastic surge—Like a pyroclastic flow, but of lower density.

radioactive (RAY dee oh AK tihv)—In the process of giving off energy or particles by the breaking apart of atoms of certain elements.

Ring of Fire—The regions of mountain-building volcanoes and earthquakes that surround the Pacific Ocean.

seismic (SYZ mihk)—Relating to vibrations in the earth, such as those caused by earthquakes.

shield volcano—A volcano with a broad, gentle slope, formed by eruptions of runny lavas that flow across the ground easily.

silica (SIH lih kuh)—A chemical combination of silicon and oxygen, and the basic ingredient of volcanic rocks.

sonar (SOH nahr, SOund NAvigation Ranging)—A method or device for detecting and locating objects, especially underwater, by mean of sound waves sent out to be reflected by the objects.

stratovolcano (STRAT oh vawl KAY noh)—A steep, conical volcano built by the eruption of lava and pyroclastic flows. A stratovolcano typically consists of more than one vent and is also called a composite volcano.

subduction zone (sub DUK shun ZOHN)—The place where two tectonic plates collide, with one plate sinking under the other.

vent—An opening in the earth's crust from which molten rock and volcanic gases escape onto the ground, into the atmosphere, or underwater.

volcanic gas (vawl KAN ihk GAS)—Gases dissolved in magma that are released into the atmosphere during eruptions. The main volcanic gases are water (steam), carbon dioxide, sulfur dioxide, and hydrogen chloride.

volcano (vawl KAY noh)—A vent at the earth's surface through which magma (molten rock), ash, and gases erupt. Also, the structure built by the eruptions.

volcanology (VAWL kuh NAH luh jee)—The scientific study of volcanoes and their products.

Further Reading

Books

Gates, Alexander E., and David Ritchie. *Encyclopedia of Earthquakes and Volcanoes*. New York: Facts on File, 2006.

Lewis, G. Brad (photographer), and Jim Kauahikaua. *Volcano: Creation in Motion*. Honolulu: Mutual Publishing, 2004.

Lopes, Rosaly. *The Volcano Adventure Guide*. Cambridge, England: Cambridge University Press, 2005.

Mallory, Kenneth. *Diving to a Deep-Sea Volcano*. New York: Houghton Mifflin, 2006.

O'Meara, Donna. *Into the Volcano: A Volcano Researcher at Work*. Toronto: Kids Can Press, 2007.

Thompson, Dick. *Volcano Cowboys: The Rocky Evolution of a Dangerous Science*. New York: St. Martin's Press, 2000.

Winchester, Simon. *Krakatoa: The Day the World Exploded: August 27, 1883*. New York: Harper Perennial, 2003.

Videos

NOVA: Volcano Under the City, WGBH Boston, 2006.

Volcano: Nature's Inferno, National Geographic, 1990.

Internet Addresses

Smithsonian Institution's Global Volcanism Program

<http://www.volcano.si.edu/index.cfm>

A wealth of information about current and historical volcanism around the world, including maps and images.

U.S. Geological Survey Volcano Hazards Program

<http://volcanoes.usgs.gov>

Provides updates about volcanic activity worldwide as well as background information about the history and science of volcanoes, videos, links to volcano observatories, and more.

Yellowstone: Monitoring the Fire Below

<http://www.amnh.org/sciencebulletins/
   ?sid=e.f.yellowstone.20060601>

The American Museum of Natural History's interactive online exhibit about the Yellowstone volcano. Includes articles, interviews, videos, and photographs.

Index